Interleaf Quick Reference

Jonathan Starr

ONWORD
PRESS

Interleaf Quick Reference
Jonathan Starr

Published by:
OnWord Press
2530 Camino Entrada
Santa Fe, NM 87505-4835 USA

Copyright © 1995 Jonathan Starr

SAN 694-0269
First Edition, 1995
10 9 8 7 6 5 4 3 2 1

Printed in the United States of America

Library of Congress Cataloging-in-Publication Data
Interleaf Quick Reference
Jonathan Starr, 1st Edition
Includes index.
1. Interleaf publisher (computer file) 2. Desktop publishing I. Title
Z253.532.I58S73 1995
686.2′2544536--dc20
94-48559

ISBN 1-56690-040-9

Trademarks

OnWord Press is a trademark of High Mountain Press, Inc. Interleaf is a registered trademark of Interleaf, Inc. Many other products and services are mentioned in this book that are either trademarks or registered trademarks of their respective companies. OnWord Press and the author make no claim to these marks.

Warning and Disclaimer

This book is designed to provide information about Interleaf 6. Every effort has been made to make this book complete and as accurate as possible; however, no warranty or fitness is implied. The information is provided on an "as-is" basis. The author and OnWord Press shall have neither liability nor responsibility to any person or entity with respect to any loss or damages in connection with or rising from the information contained in this book.

About the Author

Jonathan Starr has over twenty years' experience in the software industry. He holds a BA degree from Harvard College and a Master's degree in Engineering from Harvard University. Since 1989, he has specialized in custom applications related to Interleaf. Prior to that, he had seven years' experience in the development of large-scale newspaper publishing systems. He is currently a member of Interleaf's Partners in Document Management program.

Mr. Starr may be contacted at:

BELSOFT   (617) 484-3921
225 Cross Street
Belmont, Massachusetts 02178-4231
starr@belsoft.tiac.net

Acknowledgments

The author and OnWord Press would like to thank Vaughn Corbridge, Susan Rice, David Adler and Sheri Giles for their comments, Philip Randall and Dave Bucholtz of Interleaf for their invaluable assistance, and Kitty Kiefer and Hazel Nesbit Kiefer for their patience and support.

Book Production

This book was produced by Sandra McDougle using Interleaf 5 and 6. The cover was produced by Lynne Egensteiner, using Quark Xpress 3.11 and Adobe Photoshop 2.5.1 on a Mac Quadra.

OnWord Press

OnWord Press is dedicated to the fine art of professional documentation. In addition to the author who developed the material for this book, many members of the OnWord Press team contribute to the book that ends up in your hands. In addition to those listed below, other members who contributed to the production and distribution of this book include Frank Conforti, Jean Nichols, Joe Adams, Robin Ortiz, James Bridge, and Bob Leyba.

Dan Raker, President
Kate Hayward, Publisher
Gary Lange, Associate Publisher
David Talbott, Acquisitions Editor
Margaret Burns, Project Editor
Carol Leyba, Production Manager
Sandra McDougle, Production Editor
Janet Leigh Dick, Marketing Director
Lynne Egensteiner, Cover designer

Introduction

Welcome to Interleaf 6, the most powerful desktop publishing software developed to date. This book is intended to help you, the Interleaf user, to use the powerful user interface of Interleaf 6 efficiently and easily. It will help the novice user to learn and the experienced user to become more efficient and to troubleshoot. It is complementary to the online Help supplied with Interleaf 6.

How This Book Is Organized

Since Interleaf 6 is accessed via a Graphical User Interface, a Graphical Index is provided. This index depicts the major elements of the user interface: the menus on the menu bars and the icons on the tool bars and graphics tool palettes. Each major element is pictured, with a brief identification of the function or commands performed by each. Page numbers are listed for reference to full descriptions. This allows you to access the book in a way that closely parallels the way you use Interleaf 6.

Next is the alphabetical commands list, which lists the menu commands of Interleaf in separate entries. Since some menu selections use several dialog boxes and have many options, some commands have entries many pages long. Screen captures of dialog boxes are used throughout.

Major subfunctions are presented in their own sections: the graphics tools, color and pattern editors, the image editor, the chart editor, and the equation editor. These are cross-referenced with the alphabetical commands list to provide a complete picture of how related functions work together. An extensive subject index covers all sections.

Typographical Conventions Used

Three other typographical features you will find in this book include Notes, Tips, and Warnings.

- **Note:** Notes present important information or concepts that might otherwise be overlooked.

- **Tip:** Tips show shortcuts and hints that help you to be more productive.

- ▲ **Warning:** Warnings point out functions and procedures that could get you in trouble if you are not careful.

Names of dialog boxes are shown in *Capitalized Bold Italic*. Names of pulldown menus are Capitalized. Individual menu entries are in *Capitalized Italic*. Labels of elements of dialog boxes, such as buttons and text fields, are in **Capitalized Boldface**.

Definitions and User Interface Conventions

A *dialog box* is a screen window containing elements such as control buttons and data fields. You can operate buttons by selecting them with the mouse, and you can enter data into data fields by selecting them and then typing.

Buttons are elements of a dialog box that are either rectangular areas labeled with an icon or words within the area, or diamond shapes labeled adjacent to the shape. Each button changes its shading to show whether it is on or off. *Radio buttons* are groups of buttons of which only one can be on at a time, similar to the station selector buttons on an automobile radio. *Toggle buttons* are buttons which change from on to off, or vice versa, independently. *Control buttons* do not have on and off states, but when you select them, Interleaf 6 takes some action.

Pulldown menus are menus that appear when you click a mouse button over a certain part of a window. Interleaf 6 windows for containers (file directories) and documents have *menu bars* across the top. A menu bar contains words, such as **File** or **Edit**, which are the starting points of pulldown menus. By clicking the mouse on a word, you will obtain a menu of functions related to that word. Pulldown menus on dialog boxes are indicated by an area containing a description or data item and a downward-pointing black arrow. Clicking with the mouse in this area displays a menu of choices, from which you can select one by clicking the mouse over it.

Some control buttons appear consistently on Interleaf 6 dialog boxes and always have the same function. **Help** opens the online Help system. **Apply** puts into effect any changes you have made on the current dialog box. **Cancel** closes the dialog box, discarding any changes that have not been applied; **Cancel** changes to **Close** after an **Apply** has been done. **OK** applies any changes and closes the dialog box. Where these buttons appear on dialog boxes, their functions are not documented in the text, since they are always consistent.

Dialog boxes opened by operations within a document which have an **Apply** button often have a pulldown menu labeled Apply. This pulldown gives you three choices, which determine the effect of selecting the **Apply** button: apply changes only to the current instances, apply all changes to all objects of the same type with the same name (including the master), or copy all this instance's properties to all objects of the same type with the same name.

Dialog boxes that display the properties of components, or other objects with names, have two common control buttons that allow you to define new masters and to copy properties between masters and instances. A button labeled **New** initiates a procedure that allows you to create a new master based on the current instance. A button labeled **More** opens a menu that allows you to copy the instance's content or properties to the master, to copy the master's properties to this instance, to rename the master and its instances, or to convert the instance to a different name (another master).

Some menu entries or elements of dialog boxes are inactive under certain conditions and cannot be selected. For example, you cannot use the *Create Table* menu entry if you are not working within a table, and you cannot enter a value in the **Width** field of a variable–width microdocument. In these cases, the entry or element is still visible, but it is displayed in gray, indicating that it cannot be used at the moment.

Windows Notes

Most of the user interface of Interleaf 6 for Windows is identical to that of Interleaf 6 for Motif. Windows users will notice that the Copy and Paste icons on the document tool bar conform to Microsoft Office conventions rather than the icons depicted here. Also, dialog boxes related to printing operations and file opening/saving follow Windows conventions.

If you are using a two–button mouse, references to the middle mouse button should be interpreted to mean holding the SHIFT key down while pressing the left (select) mouse button.

Table of Contents

Graphics Tool Palettes   135

Color Palette   173

Graphical
Index

Graphical Index

The Document Tool Bar

The document tool bar is accessible at the top of every open Interleaf 6 document's window. It may be customized by each installation (see page 59). This description applies to the default (initial) appearance.

The document tool bar has two versions, the *text tool bar*, which is displayed when you are not working within a frame, and the *graphics tool bar*, which is displayed when you have a frame open. Interleaf 6 automatically changes to the appropriate tool bar as you change your working context. You can also force a change to the other tool bar at any time by selecting a tool bar icon.

The Text Tool Bar

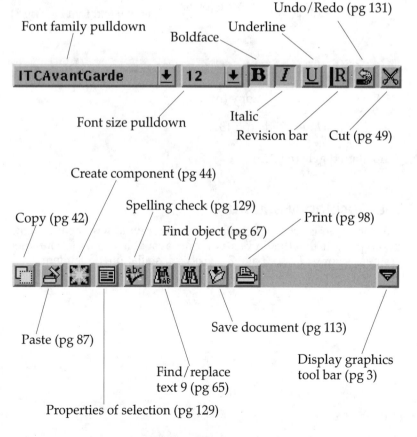

The Graphics Tool Bar

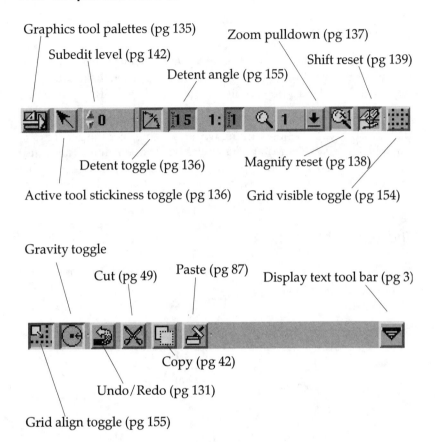

Graphics tool palettes (pg 135)   Zoom pulldown (pg 137)

Subedit level (pg 142)   Shift reset (pg 139)

Detent angle (pg 155)

Detent toggle (pg 136)   Magnify reset (pg 138)

Active tool stickiness toggle (pg 136)   Grid visible toggle (pg 154)

Gravity toggle

Cut (pg 49)   Paste (pg 87)   Display text tool bar (pg 3)

Copy (pg 42)

Undo/Redo (pg 131)

Grid align toggle (pg 155)

The Desktop Menu Bar

This menu bar is accessible from all container windows, including the desktop. Note that the *Book* entry is only available when the container is a book. For *GoTo*, see page 73. *Tools* is installation–dependent.

File

New	▶	New icon (file or container) (page 84)
Open...	Ctrl+xf	Open selected icon(s) (page 84)
Close	Ctrl+xc	Close selected icon(s) (page 25)
Import/Export...		Filter (convert) file(s) (page 76)
File Properties...		Change icon properties (page 62)
Print...	Ctrl+xp	Print icon(s) (page 98)
Print Setup...		Set up printers (page 102)
Publish...		Publish selected file(s) (page)
Exit	Ctrl+xe	Stop Interleaf 6 (page 61)

Edit

Cut	Shift+Del	Cut icon(s) to clipboard (page 49)
Copy	Ctrl+Ins	Copy icon(s) to clipboard (page 42)
Paste	Shift+Ins	Paste from clipboard (page 87)
Delete		Delete selected icon(s) (page 50)
Link		Create links to icon(s) (page 80)
Select All	Ctrl+A	Select icons in container (page 115)
Select Toggle		Select/deselect icons (page 119)
Attributes...		Change icon attributes (page 18)
Attributes Setup...		Set up attributes (page 20)

View

Full Size		Size window to fit contents (page 120)
Update	Ctrl+xu	Match with directory (page 131)
Line Up Icons		Align icons in rows (page 80)
Transpose Icons		Icons change places (page 131)
Sort Icons...		By name, type, size, date (page)
File Names		Show file system names (page 84)

Book

Index	▶	Create an index (page 77)
TOC		Create a table of contents (page 124)
A-Page	▶	Split and Join documents (pages 17, 18)
Sync		Update book information (page 123)

With no selection

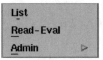

Directory listing (page 80)
Evaluate Lisp expressions (page 106)
Tool Manager (page 130)
Update Expanded Link (page 132)
Cleanup (page 25)

Change user preferences (page 87)

With a selection

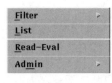

Import/export a file (page 77)
Directory listing (page 80)
Evaluate Lisp expressions (page 106)
Cleanup (page 25)
Expand link (62)

Change user preferences (page 87)

The Document Menu Bar

The document menu bar is accessible at the top of every open Interleaf 6 document's window. All entries are tear-off pulldown menus. It has two forms. The text form is displayed when there is no open frame:

The graphics form is displayed when there is an open frame:

File   Edit   View   Properties   Tools   Create   Arrange   Change

Only the text form has the Tables pulldown, and only the graphics form has the Arrange and Change pulldowns. Pulldowns that are on both forms have the same entries on each, except for Create.

File

New	▸	New file or container (page 84)
Open...	Ctrl+xf	Open another file (page 84)
Close	Ctrl+xc	Close the current document (page 25)
Save	Ctrl+xs	Save document to disk (page 113)
Save As...		Save with choice of format (page 113)
Revert to	▸	Open earlier version (page 106)
Import...		Add contents of other file (page 75)
File Properties...		Properties of document file (page 62)
Print...	Ctrl+xp	Print this document (page 98)
Print Setup...		Set up printers (page 102)
Publish...		Distribute this document (page 105)
A–Page	▸	Split and Join documents (pages 17, 18)
Exit	Ctrl+xe	Stop Interleaf 6 (page 61)

Edit

Undo Typing	Alt BkSp	Undo/Redo last change (page 131)
Cut	Shift+Del	Cut from document to clipboard (page 49)
Copy	Ctrl+Ins	Copy content to clipboard (page 42)
Paste	Shift+Ins	Paste from clipboard to (page 87)
Delete		Delete selection from document (page 50)
Duplicate		Duplicate graphics objects (page 151)
Select	▸	Select document content (page 114)
Find/Change...	Ctrl+s	Search and replace in text (page 65)
Find Object...		Search for objects in document (page 67)
Convert	▸	Case, to/from inlines, etc. (page 39)
Hyphen	▸	Change hyphenation points (page 74)
Tab Fill	▸	Change tab fill (page 124)
Delete Master...		Delete unused masters (page 50)

View

Tool Bar	Show/hide tool bar (page 130)
Rulers	Show/hide rulers (page 112)
Component Bar	Show/hide the component bar (page 25)
Component Names	Show component names (page 25)
Attribute Values...	Show component attributes (page 25)
Graphics	Display frame contents or borders (page 74)
Overlay Frames	Show/hide overlay frames (page 74)
Underlay Frames	Show/hide underlay frames (page 74)
Facing Pages	Display facing pages (page 62)
Markers...	Show/hide markers (page 81)
Zoom	Enlarge/reduce view (page 132)

Properties

Selection...	Esc ps

Properties of text or object (page 129)

Te**x**t...	Esc px

Properties of text (page 129)

Component...
Top-level components (page 30)

Inline...
Inline components (page 26)

Frame...
Open or selected frame (page 69)

Table...
Current table properties (page 125)

Row...
Current row properties (page 128)

Cell...
Current cell properties (page 126)

Attributes...
Change attributes of object (page 18)

Attributes Setup...
Define attributes (page 20)

Document...	Esc pd

Current document properties (page 51)

Microdocument...
Of *open* microdocument (page 81)

Page Number Streams...
Format page numbers (page 85)

Autonumber Streams...
Format autonumbers (page 21)

Tools

Spelling...	Ctrl+xn

Spell check text (page 121)

Shape Text...
Shape text (page 119)

Graphics
Graphics tool palettes (page 135)

Colors...
Define or modify colors (page 173)

Patterns...
Define or modify patterns (page 3)

Revision Tracking...
Control Revision Tracking (page 107)

Read–Eval...
Evaluate Lisp expressions (page 106)

Preferences...
Change user preferences (page 87)

Edit Tool Bar...
Add/change/remove icons (page 59)

Create

Component...	Esc rc

Top-level component (page 44)

Inline...
Inline component (page 45)

Autonumber...
Autonumber (page 42)

Frame...
Create a frame (page 45)

Index...	Esc rx

Create an index token (page 45)

Reference
Create references (pages 43, 45-47)

Autoreference	Esc ru

Create an autoreference (page 42)

Chart
Create a chart (page 23)

Equation
Create an equation (page 47)

Date
Enter current date in document text (page 44)

Time
Enter current time in document text (page 49)

Character
Create a character in document text (page 43)

Create text object

Create

Line	Select the line drawing tool (page 137)
Rectangle	Select the rectangle tool (page 137)
Ellipse	Select the ellipse tool (page 138)
Freehand	Select the freehand tool (page 140)
Arc ▸	Open arc menu (page 140)
Bézier ▸	Open bezier menu (page 164)
Text ▸	Open microdocument/text string menu (page 138)
Named	Select the named tool (page 140)
Chart	Select the chart tool (page 137)
Equation	Create an equation (page 141)
Group Level	Create a nested group (page 145)
Poly	Draw lines for polygon (page 145)

Create graphics object

Tables

Create Table...		Create a table (page 47)
Create Row...	Esc rr	Add row to table (page 47)
Create Column	Esc rl	Add column to table (page 44)
Change Width...		Change width of column(s) (page 24)
Select Cells ▸		Select table cells (page 115)
Join Cells		Remove a straddle (page 80)
Split Cell		Create a straddle (page 122)
Fonts ▸		Change font size of cell(s) (page 68)
Empty Cell(s)		Remove cell contents (page 61)
Select Rows ▸		Select table rows (page 117)
Split Table		Split table into two tables (page 122)
Convert Text to Table...		Convert text to table (page 41)
Edit Rulings...		Change ruling properties (page 58)

Arrange

Align ▸	Align objects to each other (page 146)
Align to Frame ▸	Align objects to the frame (page 147)
Move to Front	Bring selected objects to the front (page 148)
Move to Back	Put selected objects to the back (page 148)
Group	Create a group from selected objects (page 150)
Ungroup	Separate grouped objects (page 150)
Select/Move Tool	Select and move without resizing (page 136)
Select Tool	Select without moving or resizing (page 136)

Change

Flip ▸	Flip selected objects (page 148)
Rotate ▸	Rotate selected objects (pages 136, 136, 148)
Stretch/Shear ▸	Stretch and Shear tools (pages 138, 139)
Convert ▸	Outline, to/from iso, poly (pages 149, 149)
Select/Size/Move Tool	Select, size, and move objects (page 136)
Size to Frame ▸	Size to Frame Tools (page 147)
Bézier ▸	Bezier tools (pages 163-164)
Fill/Edge...	Fill/Edge Dialog (page 152)
Locks...	Locks Dialog (page 156)
Measurements...	Measurements Dialog (page 157)
Name...	Named Graphics Object Dialog (page 167)
Frame Settings ▸	Graphics settings dialog boxes (page 73)
Level ▸	Change the subedit level (page 144)
Close Frame	Close the open frame (page 151)

The Graphics Palettes

The Graphics Drawing Tools Palette

Selection tools (page 136)

Rotate circular/magnify (page 136)

Line tool (page 137)

Rectangle tool (page 137)

Named graphic objects tool (page 140)

Magnify tools (page 137)

Stretch tool (page 138)

Arc tools (page 140)

Ellipse tool (page 138)

Chart tool (page 137)

Shift tools (page 139)

Shear tools (page 139)

Freehand drawing tool (page 140)

Microdocument/Text String tools (page 138)

Equation tool (page 141)

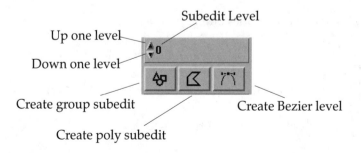

Up one level
Down one level
Subedit Level
Create group subedit
Create poly subedit
Create Bezier level

The Graphics Editing Tools Palette

 Align objects commands (page 146)

 Flip commands (page 148)

 Convert to Iso commands (page 149)

 Group and Ungroup commands (page 150)

 Duplicate command (page 151)

 Align objects to frame commands (page 147)

 Rotate by detent commands (page 148)

 Convert from Iso commands (page 149)

 Undo and Redo commands (page 150)

 Close frame command (page 151)

 Size to Frame commands (page 147)

 Front and Back commands (page 148)

 Convert to outline/poly commands (page 149)

Delete graphics object (page 150)

The Graphics Editing Tools Palette (Dialogs)

Fill/Edge dialog (page 152)

Measurements dialog (page 157)

Grid dialog (page 154)

Named graphic objects dialog (page 158)

Animation dialog (page 155)

Text dialog (page 159)

Locks dialog (page 156)

The Bezier Tools Palette

Select tools (page 163)

Shape tool (page 163)

Connect command (page 163)

Smooth/Corner point tools (page 164)

Split tool (page 164)

Straighten command (page 164)

Freehand tool (page 164)

Unlock/Lock angles commands (page 165)

Alphabetical Commands List

Alphabetical Commands List

A-page Split

ACCESS: Document menu bar: File→A-Page→Split

FUNCTION: Split a document into sections, preserving ranges of page numbers

◆ **Tip:** A-page operations are only available within books. A split must be done from within an open document.

A-page (absolute-page) splitting enables you to preserve the page numbering of a document when you add pages in the middle. The document is split into separate document files. Each document file will preserve its initial page number even if pages are added to preceding document files. When a document file grows, pages at the end are given unique numbers, but the number of the first page of the next document does not change. Each of the new document icons is given a unique name by appending a suffix to the original icon name. Each suffix indicates the initial page number(s) contained within that document file.

If the **A-Page** button of the *Page Number Streams Properties* dialog box (see page 85) is turned on, unique page numbers are added by appending an alphabetic suffix to the previous last page number. Otherwise, sequential numbers are used. The *Page Number Streams Properties* contains other A–Page number format specifications.

For example, suppose that you have a ten-page document numbered from one to ten, and you A-page split it into two five-page parts. If you then open the first part and type in new material, you will eventually add new pages to this part. If the **A-Page** button of the *Page Number Streams Properties* dialog box is on, the pages of the first document file will be numbered 1 through 5, 5a, 5b, and so on. Otherwise, they will be numbered 1 through 5, 6, 7, etc. In either case, the first page of the next document file will be numbered 6.

The File→A-Page→Split→Sheets menu choice offers you three ways to perform a split: *All*, *Current*, and *Range*. If you select *All*, the document is split into separate pages, each in its own document file. The *Current* choice splits the document into two parts, with the current page being the last page of one part. Selecting *Range* brings up two dialog boxes, in which you enter the first and last page numbers of a range. The document will be split into two or three parts, such that one of the parts begins and ends with the pages you specified. Selecting File→A-Page→Split→Range provides quicker access to the *Range* option.

◆ **Tip:** A-page splitting causes all the split parts to be saved, along with any edits that may have been pending at the time of the split.

You do not have to execute a Save to complete the split. After the split, one document will remain open. You can execute File→Revert→to Backup from this document and recover the backup version of the pre-split document.

A-page Join

ACCESS: Document menu bar: File→A-Page→Join
Desktop menu bar: Book→A-Page→Join

FUNCTION: Join A-page sections

∾ Note: A-page operations are only available within books.

This command reverses the effect of A-page splitting (see page 17) by combining two split parts into one document file.

To perform an A-page join, you must open one of the split document files and select this operation from the open document's File pulldown. The document you wish to combine with this one must be immediately before or immediately after the open document in book order.

You have two menu choices for a join: Next, which combines this document with the next, and Previous, which combines the open document with the preceding one.

The resultant document's name has a suffix that reflects the combined page number ranges. If you join all the split parts of a document, the final document has the same name as the document that was originally split.

◆ **Tip:** A-page joining causes the resultant document to be saved, along with any edits that may have been pending at the time of the join. You do not have to execute a Save to complete the join.

◆ **Tip:** After the join, one document will remain open. If you execute File→Revert→to Backup from this document, you will recover the backup version of the open document before the join. The document that was just joined to it will be lost. To avoid this, execute a split before reverting to backup, to separate the joined material again.

Attributes of icon or object in document

ACCESS: Document menu bar: Properties→Attributes
Desktop menu bar: Edit→Attributes
Component bar menu

FUNCTION: Change values of attributes

This function allows you to change the values of attributes of either an icon (desktop object) or an object, such as a component, within a document. To access from the desktop menu bar, one or more icons will be selected. Separate dialog boxes are opened for each selected icon.

An *Attributes* dialog box is opened:

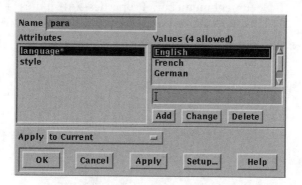

The name of the object (component, table, row, etc.) whose attribute values are being modified is displayed in the **Name** field.

⮞ **Note:** The Name field is particularly important because in all other respects, the *Attributes* dialog box looks the same for different types of objects.

The list headed **Attributes** lists all defined attributes (see page 20). Attributes having at least one value are denoted by an asterisk appended to the name in this list. To modify values for a listed attribute, select it, causing it to be highlighted. The highlighted attribute's existing values are displayed in the list headed **Values**.

The field beneath the **Values** list is where you actually make changes. In this field, the value highlighted in the **Values** list is displayed and may be modified. You can type a new value into this field and select **Add** to add a new value to the list. You can change the value displayed in the field and select **Change** to replace the highlighted value with the contents of the field. Or, you can select **Delete** to delete the corresponding listed value.

The **Setup...** button opens an *Attributes Setup* dialog box (see page 20).

Attributes setup

SELECTION: Yes

ACCESS: Desktop menu bar: Edit→Attributes Setup . . ..
Document menu bar: Properties→Attributes Setup
Attributes dialog box Setup... button

FUNCTION: Define attributes and their properties

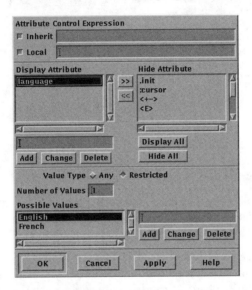

The **Inherit** and **Local** fields may be used for entry of control expressions.

The Display Attribute subwindow lists attributes that will be visible in various dialog boxes when working with the selected file. The Hide Attribute subwindow lists attributes that will not be visible.

➤ **Note:** The attributes .init, :cursor, <+->, <E>, <RevCreateDate>, <RevCreator>, <RevModifier>, and <RevModifyDate> are used for Interleaf 6 functions and should not be modified.

To create a new attribute, enter its name into the text field above the **Add, Change,** and **Delete** buttons, then select **Add.** The new name is added to the Display Attribute subwindow. Attribute names can be moved back and forth between the Display Attribute and Hide Attribute subwindows by selecting each name to be moved and then selecting the double arrows (>> and <<) that point from one subwindow to ·the other.

The **Display All** and **Hide All** buttons move all attributes to the Display Attribute or Hide Attribute subwindows, respectively.

Autonumber properties

SELECTION: Yes

ACCESS: Document text area menu: Properties

FUNCTION: Modify autonumber token properties

An *Autonumber Properties* dialog box opens:

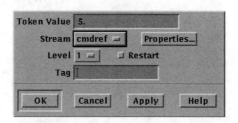

The read-only **Token Value** field shows the value of the autonumber token within its stream. This is the numeric value, regardless of the stream's formatting properties. The **Stream** pulldown allows you to move the autonumber into a different stream. **Properties** opens an *Autonumber Streams* dialog box (see below).

Level allows you to assign the autonumber to any level permitted by the stream's properties.

If **Restart** is on, this token's value is the **Starting Value** specified by the stream properties. **Tag** is an arbitrary text string (which must be unique within a book) which allows you to link references to this token, with either a tag you specify (see page 46) or an automatically generated tag (see page 42).

Autonumber Stream properties

ACCESS: Document menu bar: Properties→Autonumber Streams
        Autonumber Properties dialog box **Properties** button

FUNCTION: Define and modify autonumber streams

Autonumber streams provide automatically sequenced numbers for chapters, list items, figures, and other parts of a book or document. Each stream has its own formatting information. Autonumber streams may be exported from catalogs.

An *Autonumber Streams* dialog box is opened:

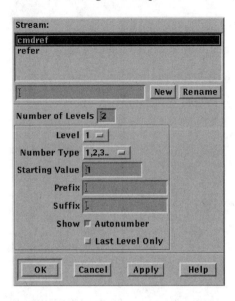

The **Stream:** list shows all currently defined autonumber streams. To change the properties of a stream, highlight the stream, select the desired property settings, and press **Apply**. To create a new stream, enter its name in the field to the left of the **New** button, and press the **New** button. To rename the stream, highlight it in the **Stream:** list, type the new name in the field to the left of the **New** button, and press the **Rename** button. The stream is renamed; all its instances will now show the new name in their properties.

The **Number of Levels** field is a number from one to 20 that defines the number of levels of nesting of this autonumber. For example, you might use a four-level stream to number chapters, subchapters, sections, and paragraphs. The **Level** pulldown selects one level's properties to display and set on the dialog box. Each level has its own independent values of the remaining fields.

The **Number Type** pulldown lets you select Arabic numerals, upper or lower case roman numerals, or upper or lower case letters to format the page number value. If you use letters, the sequence counts from A to Z, then from AA to AZ, from BA to BZ, and so on.

Starting Value is a number, defaulting to one, that defines the initial value, and restart value, of the specified level. A level restarts whenever a higher level of the same stream (with a lower **Level** number) changes value, or (for level 1) whenever an autonumber instance has the **Restart** property set.

Prefix and **Suffix** define optional text strings to be placed before and after the formatted number of the current level.

In the **Show** section, if **Autonumber** is off, autonumbers at this level (as specified on the autonumber's property sheet) will not be visible at all, though they may still be the targets of visible autonumber references. If **Autonumber** is on, autonumbers at this level will be visible; if **Last Level Only** is on, only the current level will be visible.

For example, suppose you have chapters, subchapters, sections, and paragraphs numbered in a four-level stream. You would have chapters numbered with level one autonumbers. Subchapters would be numbered with level two autonumbers. Sections would have level three autonumbers, and you might have **Last Level Only** turned off. Then, section C in subchapter 1 of chapter VII might have a visible number such as "VII-1.C," where the punctuation is supplied by the **Prefix** and **Suffix** fields. Paragraphs would be level four autonumbers, and you might turn **Last Level Only** on. Then, in section C in subchapter 1 of chapter VII, paragraph b could be labeled "b." If **Last Level Only** were off, that paragraph might by labeled "VII-1.C.b."

◆ **Tip:** You can include autonumbers in the prefixes of components, as is often done with chapter heads or list items. If you have punctuation that you wish to appear with the autonumbers in the prefixes, it is often better to include the punctuation as a separate part of the prefix, rather than specifying it in the **Prefix** and **Suffix** fields. This allows you to use different (or no) punctuation when including references to the autonumber in the body of your text. For example, suppose you want chapters to be labeled "B. Pricing," where "B" is the autonumber value. If you make the period following the "B" a separate part of the prefix, then in your text you can say "Refer to Chapter B, where this is described...." If you make the period a **Suffix** to the autonumber, you cannot prevent it from also appearing in the reference.

Change width of table columns

ACCESS: Document menu bar: Tables→Change Width
            Document Tables menu

FUNCTION: Change widths of columns in a table

A *Change Column Width* dialog box is opened:

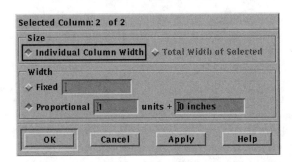

The **Selected Column** line tells you which columns are selected. You can select any one column by clicking the left mouse button in any cell of that column. You can select a range of columns by clicking the left mouse button in any cell of the left-most of those columns, then clicking the middle mouse button in a cell of the right-most column. Any change width operation affects all selected columns.

Column widths are either fixed or proportional. Fixed widths change only when explicitly changed, such as through this dialog box. Proportional widths change whenever the table as a whole changes width or when other columns within the table change size. Fixed widths are in terms of fixed units of measure (inches, centimeters, etc.). Proportional widths are in terms of units whose ratios relate the sizes of the columns to each other. Proportional-width and fixed-width columns may be combined in one table.

In a table created from scratch, all columns have proportional widths with a unit value of one.

If you select the **Fixed** radio button, you can enter fixed widths in the field to the right. If you also select **Individual Column Width**, the value you enter will become the width of each of the selected columns, which therefore will all have the same width. If you select **Fixed** and **Total Width of Selected**, all selected columns will become narrower or wider, preserving their proportional relationships, so that their total width becomes the value you entered. If you enter fixed widths that would be too wide for the page, the entry will be rejected.

If you select the **Proportional** radio button, you can enter a proportional width value for all selected columns. No matter what value you enter, all selected columns will end up with the same width, even if they had different widths to begin with. They may change width in relation to other columns.

The fixed-units field to the right of the proportional units field allows you to enter a fixed amount to be added to the proportionally determined column width. If you enter a fixed amount that would be too wide for the page, the entry will be rejected.

➥ **Note:** Proportional units can have fractional amounts, allowing you to precisely adjust the ratios of sizes. Remember that the meaning of a proportional width unit is determined by the sum of proportional widths of all columns.

Cleanup directory

ACCESS: Desktop menu bar: Tools→Admin→Cleanup
           Desktop Tools menu

FUNCTION: Purge backup files in a container

All backup files created by Interleaf 6 in the current container are deleted.

Close window

ACCESS: Desktop menu bar: File→Close
           Document menu bar: File→Close

FUNCTION: Close an open window (container, file, or document)

The current window is closed. If it is the only open container window, and no unmodified files are open under Interleaf 6, Interleaf 6 terminates execution and all its windows are closed. You are given a chance to confirm or cancel before Interleaf terminates execution.

Component bar visibility

ACCESS: Document menu bar: View→Component Bar

FUNCTION: Hide/show document component bar

If this menu item is selected directly, the component bar in the current document is hidden if it is visible, and made visible if it is hidden.

This menu item also has two subitems: **Component Names** and **Attribute Values**. If **Component Names** is selected, the component bar is made visible and component names are displayed in it.

If **Attribute Values** is selected, a *Select Attribute* dialog box is opened:

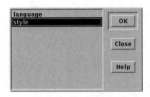

If the operator selects one of the displayed attributes and then selects **OK**, the value of the selected attribute is displayed in the component bar for each component.

Component properties (inline)

ACCESS: Document menu bar: Properties→Inline. . .
Document text menu

FUNCTION: Change properties of an inline component

An *Inline Component Properties* dialog box opens. This dialog box has three pages, each corresponding to a radio button with one of these labels: **Basic Text**, **Advanced Text**, and **Format**.

Inline Component Text Properties (basic)

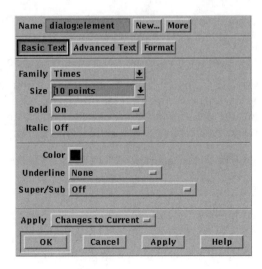

The Family pulldown lists the available font families, and allows you to select a new default font for the current component. The Size pulldown lists available sizes up to 36 point. By placing the cursor directly in the **Size** field, you can enter a size between 2 and 200 points.

Text properties **Bold** and **Italic** are controlled by pulldowns. On these pulldowns, *Off* turns the property off within the inline, and *On* turns it on. *Inherit Same* causes it to be the same as the corresponding property of the enclosing component (inline or top-level). *Inherit Opposite* causes it to have the opposite value from the corresponding property of the enclosing component.

The Color pulldown brings up a *Color* dialog box for inline components:

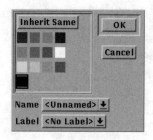

This dialog box works just as described for other *Color* dialog boxes (see page 178) with the addition of the **Inherit Same** button. If you select this button, the inline component takes the color property of the enclosing component, whether top-level or inline.

The Underline pulldown offers *None* for no underlining within the inline, *Single* for single underline, and *Double* for double underline. *Inherit Same* causes it to be the same as the underline property of the enclosing component. *Inherit Increase* causes it to have a higher value than the underline property of the enclosing component, that is, single underline if the enclosing component has none, double underline if the enclosing component has single. *Inherit Decrease* causes it to have a lower value than the underline property of the enclosing component, that is, no underline if the enclosing component has single, and single underline if the enclosing component has double.

Both the superscript and subscript properties (which are mutually exclusive) are controlled by the Super/Sub pulldown. On this pulldown, *Off* turns both properties off, *Superscript* turns subscript off and superscript on, and *Subscript* turns superscript off and subscript on. *Inherit Same (sub)* causes the subscript property to be inherited from the enclosing component (if on, the superscript property is turned off). *Inherit Same (super)* causes the superscript property to be inherited from the enclosing component (if on, the subscript property is turned off). *In-*

herit Opposite (sub) and *Inherit Opposite (super)* cause the specified properties to be set to the opposite of the corresponding property in the enclosing component.

Inline Component Text Properties (advanced)

Strikethrough, **Overbar**, **Rev Bars**, and **Pair Kerning** are all controlled by similar pulldowns. *Off* turns the property off within the inline, and *On* turns it on. *Inherit Same* causes it to be the same as the corresponding property of the enclosing component (inline or top-level). *Inherit Opposite* causes it to have the opposite value from the corresponding property of the enclosing component.

Capitalization (**Caps**) can be *As Typed*, *Small Cap* (first letter), *All Small Caps*, *All Capitals*, or *Inherit Same*. The *As Typed* choice reverts to the operator-entered capitalization. *Inherit Same* causes the capitalization property to be the same as that of the enclosing component.

◆ **Tip:** Interleaf 6 "remembers" what you typed even after you save and close the document. You can always recover the capitalization as you typed it by selecting *As Typed*.

Dictionary lists all available dictionaries as well as *<No Dictionary>*. *Inherit* causes this property to be inherited from the enclosing component.

Track Kerning may be *Off* or have any of three values of looseness or three values of tightness. In addition, you may select *Inherit Same*, *Inherit Tighter*, or *Inherit Looser*, to cause the current inline's track kerning to be the same as or tighter or looser than that of the enclosing component.

Inline Component Format Properties

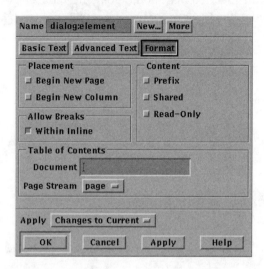

The **Begin New Page** toggle button forces the inline to the top of a page, starting a new page if necessary. The **Begin New Column** button forces the inline to the top of a column, beginning a new column (and possibly a new page) if necessary. The inline will not necessarily be the first text on the new page or column.

The **Allow Breaks Within Inline** button determines whether or not column or page breaks are desirable within this inline. If this property is off, Interleaf 6 will try to keep all of this inline in the same column and page (which may force a column or page break).

Three toggle buttons control whether or not the inline has a **Prefix**, whether or not it is **Shared** (all content shared by all instances), or **Read-Only** (cannot be edited by typing, cutting, pasting, etc.).

The **Table of Contents** field allows you to enter a TOC document name. This causes the current inline to be included in the specified Table of Contents (see page 124). The Page Stream pulldown allows you to select from a list of page number streams for formatting a TOC entry.

▲ **Warning:** Do not use a TOC document name that conflicts with the name of a document already in the book, or your document will be overwritten by a TOC document when you perform Table of Contents generation.

◆ **Tip:** If you want to include part of an inline component's content in a TOC entry, but not all of it, do not apply the Table of Contents field to that inline component. Instead, create (or convert to) a nested inline *within* that inline component, so that the nested inline contains the material that should go in the Table of Contents. Use the nested inline to generate the TOC entry.

Component properties (top level)

ACCESS: Document menu bar: Properties→Component
Component bar menu

FUNCTION: Change properties of top-level components

A *Component Properties* dialog box opens. This dialog box has six pages, each corresponding to a radio button with one of these labels: **Text**, **Format**, **Content**, **Page**, **Composition**, and **Tabs**.

Component Text Properties

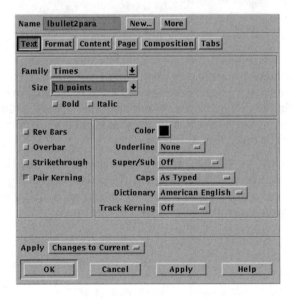

The Family pulldown lists the available font families and allows you to select a new default font for the current component. The Size pulldown lists available sizes up to 36 point. By placing the cursor directly in the **Size** field, you can enter a size between 2 and 200 points.

The **Color** button brings up a *Color* dialog box (see page 178). Text properties **Bold**, **Italic**, **Rev Bars**, **Overbar**, **Strikethrough**, and **Pair**

Kerning are controlled by toggle buttons. The **Underline** pulldown offers a choice of *None*, *Single*, and *Double*. The **Super/Sub** pulldown offers a choice of *Superscript*, *Subscript*, or *Off* (neither).

Capitalization (**Caps**) can be *As Typed*, *Small Cap* (first letter), *All Small Caps*, or *All Caps*. The *As Typed* choice reverts to the operator-entered capitalization, even if this menu was used to change the component property and the document was then saved and closed.

The Dictionary pulldown lists available dictionaries and <No Dictionary>. **Track Kerning** may be *Off* or have any of three values of looseness or three values of tightness.

Component Format Properties

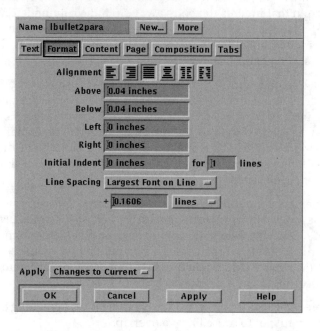

The alignment property, accessed by selecting the **Format** button, is set by six graphical radio buttons:

The component is *flush left*.

The component is *flush right*.

The component is *justified* (filled to both left and right, if possible).

The component is *centered*.

If the document has a two-sided page layout align the component to the *inner* margin.

If the document has a two-sided page layout, align the component to the *outer* margin.

The component's margins are defined in the **Above, Below, Left,** and **Right** fields. The two fields **Initial indent** and **for ... lines** allow you to specify a left indent effective for a certain number of text lines.

◆ **Tip:** By coordinating the left margin, tab properties, and initial indent, you can create "hanging indent" effects in which some initial content is to the left of the paragraph body. Define a negative initial indent that spaces the initial content away from the body, a left margin that indents the body away from the column left margin, and a tab that reaches from the initial content to the body. Enter the initial content followed by a tab, and then enter the body. The initial content and tab may be set up as a prefix.

◆ **Tip:** The **Left,** and **Right** margins may be set using the horizontal ruler in the document window (see page 112). The margin positions are indicated on the ruler by inverted black arrowheads, which may be selected with the mouse and dragged. The **Initial indent** position is marked by a boldface letter **I** and may also be dragged. It will move whenever the right margin changes, since the initial indent is measured from the right margin.

The Line Spacing pulldown offers a choice of two measures to determine the spacing between text lines: *Largest Font on Line* and *Component Font Size*. The data field in this group lets you enter a fixed amount to add to the font-related spacing. This amount may be either in terms of lines (i.e., the vertical extent of a line), or in terms of a fixed unit. The associated pulldown gives you a choice of *Lines* or a unit.

◦ **Note:** The fixed spacing field may be negative, tightening the text. Be careful not to cause lines to overlap.

Component Content Properties

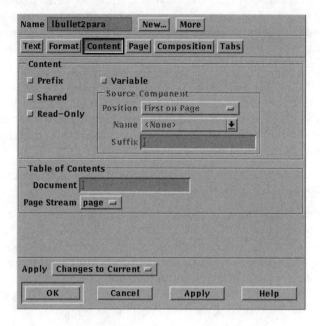

Three toggle buttons control whether or not the component has a **Prefix**, whether or not it is **Shared** (all content shared by all instances), or **Read-Only** (cannot be edited by typing, cutting, pasting, etc.).

⊷ Note: Read-Only components can still be cut from the document.

If the **Variable** button is on, this top-level component is a variable-content component. This means that its content is taken from the content of another component that occurs earlier in the document. The name of the component that provides the content must be selected from the Name pulldown in the **Source Component** area. The text content of the nearest preceding source component is copied to this component. The source component's prefix, if any, is included in the copied content. Any frames in the source are omitted. If the **Suffix** field contains text, this text is appended to the copied content. The source component may be an inline.

⊷ Note: The nearest preceding component matching the specified source name is used. Therefore, variable content components naming the same source component can have different contents at different points in the document. This can be useful in defining variable content in headers and footers. For example, by making chapter titles and subtitles the sources of variable content components, and placing the variable content components in headers and footers, you can have the current chapter and subchapter name displayed on each page. Each variable content component in a header or footer will take its content from the first source component on the same page, if any. Therefore, chapter titles and subtitles will be up to date.

◆ **Tip:** If the top-level source components contain any content, such as autonumbers, that you wish to omit from the headers or footers, you can define inlines containing the content you wish to display, and use the inlines as sources for variable content components in the headers and footers.

Variable content components are always read-only and cannot be prefix or shared content.

• **Note:** If you make a component variable content, any previous content of that component disappears. The only way to recover this content is to select Edit→Undo Properties on the document menu bar before carrying out any other editing operations. Turning off variable content makes the component editable but does not recover the original content. Any original prefix can be restored by turning the prefix property back on.

The **Table of Contents** field allows you to enter a TOC document name. This causes the current component to be included in the specified Table of Contents (see page 124). The TOC Page Number Stream pulldown allows you to select from a list of page number streams for formatting a TOC entry.

◆ **Tip:** If you want to include part of a top–level component's content in a TOC entry, but not all of it, do not apply the Table of Contents field to the component. Instead, create (or convert to) an inline within the top–level component, so that the inline contains the material that should go in the Table of Contents. Use the inline to generate the TOC entry.

▲ **Warning:** Do not use a TOC document name that conflicts with the name of a document already in the book, or your document will be overwritten by a TOC document when you perform Table of Contents generation.

Component Page Properties

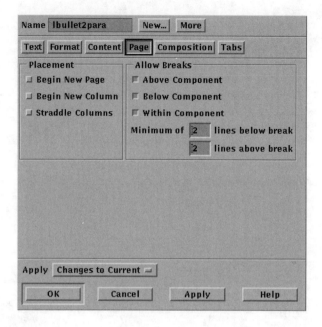

In the **Placement** section, the **Begin New Page** toggle button forces the component to the top of a page, starting a new page if necessary. The **Begin New Column** button forces the component to the top of a column, beginning a new column (and possibly a new page) if necessary. The **Straddle Columns** button allows the component to stretch all the way across a multi-column page.

In the **Allow Breaks** section, buttons and fields define composition parameters that Interleaf 6 will try to observe, although it may not be possible to do so in some cases. **Above Component**, if off, specifies that the component should be on the same page as the preceding component. **Below Component**, if off, specifies that the next component should be on the same page as the end of this component. **Within Component**, if off, specifies that all of this component should be in the same column and page (which may force a column or page break). The **Minimum of ... lines below/above break** fields specify the minimum number of text lines at the beginning or end of this component that should be isolated from the rest of the component by a column (or page) break.

◆ **Tip:** Turning off breaks **Below Component** is generally a good idea for section heads, since it is better to move a heading to a new page or column than to isolate it from the following material.

Component Composition Properties

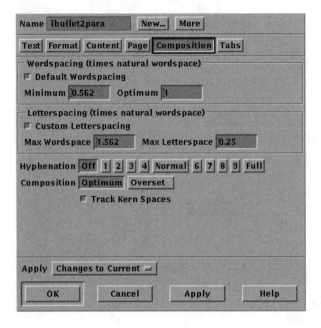

Interleaf 6 allows you to control composition by specifying two kinds of spacing within the text, wordspacing and letterspacing.

The fields in the **Wordspacing** section allow you to define the spacing permitted between words. The **Optimum** field is a multiplier; the larger it is, the further apart words will be. Interleaf 6 will try to use the spacing determined by this field. The **Minimum** field defines a wordspace that Interleaf 6 will not go below. Minimum wordspacing applies only to justified text (see page 31).

The **Default Wordspacing** button restores default wordspace settings.

Letterspacing is the spacing between letters within the same word. It applies only to justified text (see page 31). The **Custom Letterspacing** toggle button turns letterspacing on or off. If it is on, the **Max Word-space** sets the upper limit of spaces allowed between words, and the **Max Letterspace** limits the spacing between letters. Both are multipliers; the larger they are, the looser (more spread out) the text will be.

The **Hyphenation** section consists of eleven radio buttons. The one to the far left, **Off**, completely prevents hyphenation. The middle one, **Normal**, allows a moderate amount of hyphenation. The one on the far right, **Full**, allows a great deal of hyphenation. The numbered buttons allow you to select intermediate levels between **Off** and **Normal** or between **Normal** and **Full**. The less hyphenation you allow, the greater the chance that your text will have excessive white space between words or have a ragged right margin. The narrower the column, the more significant this is.

The two **Composition** radio buttons allow you further control over how tightly your text is fitted. **Optimum** means that composition is guided closely by optimum wordspacing. **Overset** means that text is packed as tightly as possible without violating the minimum wordspacing.

If the **Track Kern Spaces** button is selected, the space between words will be tightened according to the track kerning values of the appropriate font(s).

Component Tab Properties

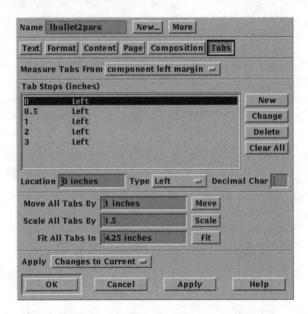

This page of the *Component Properties* dialog box allows you to add, change, and delete tab stops.

The Measure Tabs From pulldown allows you to determine the position from which the **Location** values take effect: the left margin of the component or the left edge of the column.

The **Tab Stops** list displays all tab stops currently defined for this component. Select a tab stop by highlighting it in this list; its properties are displayed in the **Location** field and Type pulldown. You can then delete the selected stop, change its properties, or create a new stop.

The **Delete** button deletes the selected tab stop.

To change a tab stop's properties, select it, and then use the **Location** field and Type pulldown to enter new properties. Select the **Change** button to use the new properties.

To define a new stop, modify the properties displayed, and select **New**. The new stop appears in the proper position within the **Tab Stops** list.

The **Clear All** button deletes all tab stops defined for this component.

⇒ **Note:** Even though you have pressed the **Delete**, **Change**, **New**, or **Clear All** buttons, the operations do not take effect until you select the **Apply** or **OK** button.

◆ **Tip:** Tab stops may be set using the horizontal ruler in the document window (see page 112). Tab positions are indicated on the ruler by upward–pointing arrows, which may be selected with the mouse and dragged. A new tab stop may be created by clicking the select button over the desired location on the ruler.

Types of Tab Stops

Left	Material to the right of the tab is left-aligned to the position of the tab stop
Right	Material to the right of the tab is positioned so that the right edge of the material is aligned at the position of the tab stop
Center	Material to the right of the tab is horizontally centered around the tab stop
Numeric	Material to the right of the tab is positioned so that the right edge of the material is aligned at the position of the tab stop as long as numeric data is entered
Decimal	Material to the right of the tab is positioned so that "decimal points," as specified by the **Decimal Char** field, are vertically aligned

If the Type pulldown specifies a decimal tab, the **Decimal Char** field specifies the character to use as the "decimal point."

The **Move All Tabs By** field and **Move** button allow you to add a fixed increment (possibly negative) to the **Location** properties of all tabs. With the **Scale All Tabs By** field and **Scale** button, you can apply a multiplier to the **Location** properties of all tabs. If you select **Fit, Location** values will be scaled up or down so that all the tab stops fit within the width in the **Fit All Tabs In** field (when you open this property sheet, the initial value in this field corresponds to the current set of tab definitions).

Convert document content

SELECTION: Yes

ACCESS: Document menu bar: Edit→Convert

FUNCTION: Convert text content (case, returns, to/from inlines)

This menu choice allows various modifications to existing content in the current document's text area. It brings up a submenu of the following choices: *lower case, UPPER CASE, Initial Upper Case, Delete Returns, Insert Returns, Remove Rev Bars, from Rev Cut, from Inline,* and *to Inline.*

Any changes made using this menu item may be reversed with **Undo** (see page 131).

lower case	The selected text is converted to lower case
UPPER CASE	The selected text is converted to upper case
Initial Upper Case	The first character of each word in the selected text is made upper case, and the rest of the text is made lower case
Delete Returns	All hard returns in the selected text are deleted
Insert Returns	Hard returns are inserted in the selected text wherever there are soft (composed) returns. This does not change line breaks. Hard returns are *not* inserted at hyphenation points
Remove Rev Bars	This operation requires a top-level component or row selection. Revision bars are removed from the selected component(s)

From Rev Cut	There must be a Revision Tracking deletion inline selected, that is, material that has been cut or deleted with Revision Tracking enabled, so that the material remains in the document but is marked as deleted. Executing this menu choice reverses the deletion, turning the selected material back into ordinary text.

↔ **Note:** You can convert multiple deletions in one operation. No harm is done if other material is also selected. The conversion will include all deletion inlines whose inline heads are selected.

From Inline	This menu choice does nothing unless there is at least one inline head (the inline marker at the beginning of the inline) selected. Each inline whose head lies within the text selection is converted from an inline into text content. This operation is carried out only at the top level within the selection, that is, any nested inlines remain inlines. By repeatedly selecting and converting the same material, all nested inlines can be converted.
to Inline	See the description immediately below

Convert to Inline:

A *Component Name Selection* dialog box is opened:

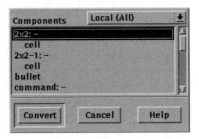

If the operator selects **Convert**, the selected material will be converted to an inline component with the highlighted name. This is equivalent to cutting the selection, creating the inline in the same position, and pasting within the inline.

Convert text to table

SELECTION: Yes

ACCESS: Document menu bar: Tables→Convert Text to Table

FUNCTION: Convert document text content to a table

There must be a text selection. A *Table Name Selection* dialog box is opened:

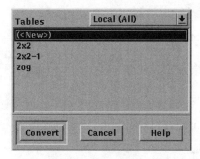

The operator may create a new table master or use an existing master. To create a new master, highlight (**<New>**) and select **Convert**. A new master will be created. The first master so created will be named Cnv, the second, Cnv-1, and so on. Each line of the text selection will become a row of the new table. Each tab in the selection will become a column boundary. Thus, the number of columns in the new master will be the largest number of tabs on a line in the selection plus one. Lines with fewer tabs will be filled out with horizontal straddles at the right side.

To use an existing master, highlight its name and select **Convert**. Each line of the text selection will become a row of the new table. Each tab in the selection will become a column boundary. The operation will not be allowed unless the text selection and the master agree on the number of columns.

If only part of the text in a component is selected, that text will be removed from the component, and the table will be placed immediately following the component. If you convert all the text of a component to a table, the component will cease to exist. The selection may include material from multiple top-level components; it will all be combined into a single table.

The presence of inlines in the selected text does not affect conversion to a table. In effect, all inlines are converted to top-level text before the conversion. If inlines are selected, you will be given a chance to confirm or cancel before anything is done.

The conversion will not be allowed if the selection contains frames or tables. If there are autonumbers, autonumber references, or page reference tokens selected, they will be preserved within the table cells.

Copy icon

SELECTION: Yes

ACCESS: Desktop menu bar: Edit→Copy
                Desktop menu

FUNCTION: Copy selected icons (files)

Copies are made of the selected icon(s) and placed on the clipboard.

Copy from document text area

SELECTION: Yes

ACCESS: Document menu bar: Edit→Copy
                Component bar menu
                Document text menu
                Text Tool Bar

FUNCTION: Copy selected document content

The selected material in the body of the current document is copied to the clipboard as a document. This material can then be pasted into the body of the same or another document, or pasted directly into an open container as a document. If the material is pasted into the component bar of a document, one or top-level components will be created, corresponding to the top-level component(s) from which the material was copied.

Create autonumber in document

ACCESS: Document Menu bar: Create→Autonumber. . .
                Document text menu

FUNCTION: Create an autonumber

A *Create Text Area Object* dialog box is opened (see page 47). The **Autonumbers** radio button is selected.

Create autoreference

SELECTION: Yes

ACCESS: Desktop menu bar: Create pulldown
                Document text menu

FUNCTION: Create a reference to an autonumber

There must be an autonumber selected in the current document, and it must be the only element of the text selection. If the autonumber does not have a tag, it is given an automatically generated tag. A reference to the autonumber is created and placed on the clipboard. It can then be pasted into the current document or a different document.

The new reference displays the autonumber value of the selected autonumber. The reference's properties may be changed by selecting it and then selecting Properties→Selection... on the document menu bar.

Create blank page number reference in document

ACCESS: Document menu bar: Create→Reference→Blank Page Number
Document text menu

FUNCTION: Create a reference to a page number

A current page reference is created at the position of the text caret.

Create character in document text

ACCESS: Document menu bar: Create→Character

FUNCTION: Create a character from a menu or palette

A submenu opens, listing specific characters: bullet, hyphen, spaces and dashes of various widths, and copyright and trademark symbols. Selecting any of these characters inserts it at the current position of the text caret. The character selected may require a specific font, such as Symbols; if it does, following the new character, the font will revert to the font you were using before selecting this menu item.

This submenu also offers **Other...** as a menu choice. This brings up a character palette:

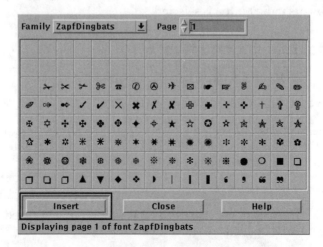

The Family pulldown lists the available font families. The palette displays a matrix of characters available in each family. Clicking on a character, and then selecting **Insert**, (or simply double–clicking on the character) inserts the character at the current position of the text caret. The font following the new character reverts to the font you were using before the insertion. The **Page** arrows permit you to page through the available pages for each font family.

Create column in table

ACCESS: Document menu bar: Ta<u>b</u>les→<u>C</u>reate Column

FUNCTION: Add a column to a table

The text cursor must be within a table.

A new column is created in the current table, with a proportional width of one. If any columns are selected, the new column is inserted to the left of the left-most selected column. Otherwise, if the text cursor is a gray right arrow (indicating a microdocument edit), the new column is placed to the left of the column containing the cursor, and if the cursor is a black triangle, the new column is placed to the right of the column containing the cursor.

Create component in document

ACCESS: Document menu bar: <u>C</u>reate→<u>C</u>omponent

FUNCTION: Create a top-level component

A *Create Text Area Object* dialog box is opened (see page 47). The **Components** radio button is selected.

Create date in document text

ACCESS: Document menu bar: <u>C</u>reate→<u>D</u>ate

FUNCTION: Enter current date in document

A submenu opens, showing the current date in a number of formats. By selecting an entry from the submenu, you insert the formatted date in the document at the current position of the text caret.

• **Note:** If there is a text selection, the date replaces the selection.

• **Note:** The date is inserted as editable text; it is not updated if the document is opened on a later date.

Create frame in document

ACCESS: Document menu bar: Create→Frame
                       Document text menu

FUNCTION: Create a graphics frame

A *Create Text Area Object* dialog box is opened (see page 47). The **Frames** radio button is selected.

Create icon

ACCESS: Desktop menu bar: File→New→(submenu)

FUNCTION: Create an icon (file or directory)

See **New Icon** on page 84.

Create index

ACCESS: Document menu bar: Create pulldown
                       Document text menu

FUNCTION: Create an entry in an index

This menu choice allows you to create index tokens. An *Index Token Properties* dialog box is opened (see page 78). If there is no text selection, this dialog box is initialized with first-level headings of ****Empty****. You can use all of the facilities described for the dialog box, including automatic insertion of fields from existing index tokens and drag and drop between fields, to create a new index entry.

➷ **Note:** If text is selected in the current document, this text becomes the initial content of the first-level headings. Any frames in the selection are ignored, even if they contain text.

Create inline component in document

ACCESS: Desktop menu bar: Create pulldown
                       Document text menu

FUNCTION: Create an inline component

A *Create Text Area Object* dialog box is opened (see page 47). The **Inlines** radio button is selected.

Create page number reference in document

ACCESS: Document menu bar: Create pulldown
                       Document text menu
                       Create→Reference→Page Number

FUNCTION: Create a page number reference

A *Create Text Area Object* dialog box is opened (see page 47). The **Page Numbers** radio button is selected.

Create reference to attribute

ACCESS: Document menu bar: Create→Reference→Attributes
             Document text menu

FUNCTION: Create an attribute reference

A *Create Attribute Reference* dialog box is opened:

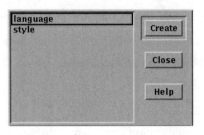

This dialog box displays a list of defined attributes. Select one and then press **Create** to create a reference. The reference is inserted in the text at the current text cursor position.

Create reference to autonumber

ACCESS: Document menu bar: Create→Reference→Autonumber
             Document text menu

FUNCTION: Create a reference to an autonumber

An autonumber reference is created at the position of the text cursor, and an *Autonumber Reference* dialog box is opened:

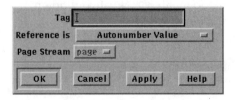

Enter the tag of an existing autonumber in the **Tag** field. The autonumber whose tag you enter must be in the current document or within a book that also contains the current document at some level. Until you enter a valid tag, the reference will be displayed as NO TAG.

When you have entered a valid tag, the reference will be displayed as either the autonumber's token value, defined according to the autonumber's stream properties, or the number of the page the autonumber is on. Which value is displayed is determined by the Reference is pulldown on the dialog box. This pulldown offers two choices: **Autonumber Value** and **Autonumber Page Location**. If **Autonumber Page Location** is selected, the Page Stream pulldown is active and lists all available page number streams for formatting the reference.

Create table in document

ACCESS: Document menu bar: Tables→Create Table. . .

FUNCTION: Create a table

A *Create Text Area Object* dialog box is opened (see page 47). The **Tables** radio button is selected.

Create table page number reference in document

ACCESS: Document menu bar: Create→Reference→Table Page Number
             Document tables menu

FUNCTION: Create a reference to a table page number

A table page reference is created at the position of the text caret.

Create table row in document

ACCESS: Document menu bar: Tables→Create Row

FUNCTION: Add a row to a table

A *Create Text Area Object* dialog box is opened (see page 47). The **Table Rows** radio button is selected.

Create text area object in document

ACCESS: Create menus
             Text Tool Bar

FUNCTION: Create objects in document text area

This dialog box is used to create top-level and inline components, frames, page number tokens, tables, table rows, and autonumbers within the current document. Each type of object is represented by a radio button on the dialog box:

Select the type of object you wish to create. A list of names (masters) for objects of this type is displayed. Highlight the desired name, and press **Create**. Objects other than top-level components are created at the position of the text caret. Top-level components are created at the position of the component bar cursor.

As you change object types, the last master used in each case is remembered and becomes the default when you change back to that type.

The pulldown menu labeled **List** lists the sources for the lists of masters displayed for selection. Possible settings are:

Local (In Use)	All masters currently in use in the document under edit are displayed
Local (All)	All currently available masters are displayed
The name of a catalog	All masters available by export from the named catalog are displayed

As you select different types of objects using the radio buttons, the **List** setting for each type of object is preserved.

◆ **Tip:** If you tend to use components or other masters in groups, or if some are used infrequently depending on the current document context, you can organize convenient groups in different catalogs. You can then select the desired catalog to control the contents of the list. In the same way, you can separate components that are generally used as inlines from those that are generally used as top-level components, so that the **Components** and **Inlines** lists contain only the appropriate entries.

The pulldown menu labeled Level is used only when the **Autonumber** radio button is selected. Use it to choose the level of autonumber you wish to create, within the levels defined for the selected master.

Some operations using the *Create Text Area Object* dialog box are context-sensitive. For example, most objects cannot be created within the top level of a table (although they may be created within a table cell), whereas table rows can only be created within a table.

The **Convert** button is enabled only for top-level components, including table rows. If you select this button, all currently selected components or rows are converted to the type selected in this dialog box.

Create time in document text

ACCESS: Document menu bar: Create→Time

FUNCTION: Enter the current time of day in a document

A submenu opens, showing the current time of day in two formats. By selecting an entry from the submenu, you insert the formatted time in the document at the current position of the text caret.

∾ **Note:** If there is a text selection, the time replaces the selection.

∾ **Note:** The time is inserted as editable text; it is not updated if the document is opened at a later time or date.

Cut icon

SELECTION: Yes

ACCESS: Desktop menu bar: Edit→Cut
              Desktop menu

FUNCTION: Cut selected icons (files)

The selected icon(s) are cut to the clipboard.

Cut from document text area

SELECTION: Yes

ACCESS: Document menu bar: Edit→Cut
              Component bar menu
              Document text menu
              ✂ Text Tool Bar

FUNCTION: Cut selected document content

The selected material in the body of the current document is removed from the current document and placed on the clipboard as a document. This material can then be pasted into the body of the same or another document, or pasted directly into an open container as a document.

Any changes made using this menu item may be reversed with **Undo** (see page 131).

Delete icon

SELECTION: Yes

ACCESS: Desktop menu bar: Edit→Delete
Desktop menu

FUNCTION: Delete icons (files)

The selected icons(s) are deleted from the file system.

▲ **Warning:** The icons are not placed on the clipboard and are not recoverable.

Delete from document text area

SELECTION: Yes

ACCESS: Document menu bar: Edit→Delete
Component bar menu
Document text menu

FUNCTION: Delete document content

The selected material in the body of the current document is removed from the current document.

Any changes made using this menu item may be reversed with **Undo** (see page 131).

∞ **Note:** Unlike **Cut**, this operation does not place the removed material on the clipboard. It cannot be pasted, and can only be recovered with **Undo**.

Delete master from document

ACCESS: Document menu bar: Edit→Delete Master

FUNCTION: Delete master definitions from document

This menu choice allows unused masters to be deleted from the current document. A *Delete Masters* dialog box is opened:

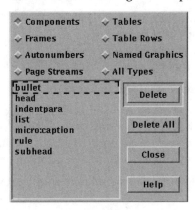

Select one of the master types listed, or **All Types** to delete all unused masters at once. If a specific type is selected, all unused master names of that type will be listed. Individual ones may be highlighted and deleted by selecting **Delete**. All the listed masters may be deleted by selecting **Delete All**.

If **All Types** is selected, **<All Unused Masters>** is displayed instead of a list, and the **Delete** button is inactive. Select **Delete All** to delete all unused masters in the document.

Only masters defined within a document can be deleted from that document's Edit menu. Masters imported from a catalog must be deleted from the catalog's Edit menu.

➥ **Note:** Deleted masters cannot be recovered.

Document Properties

ACCESS: Document menu bar: Properties→Document. . .

FUNCTION: Change document properties, including page properties

A *Document Properties* dialog box is opened. This dialog box has five pages, selected by labeled radio buttons at the top of each box.

➥ **Note:** All pages of this dialog box are inactive whenever a micro-document is open in the current document.

Document Layout Properties

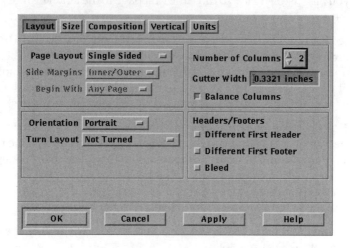

The Page Layout pulldown allows you to determine whether pages are *Single-Sided* or printed on both sides. Double-sided pages can be *Odd*

Page Left or *Odd Page Right*, depending on whether you want odd-numbered pages to the left or right of the crease.

Side Margins is active when **Page Layout** is double-sided. You can choose *Left/Right*, meaning that the page margins are for the left and right side of each page, regardless of whether it is a left-hand or right-hand page. Or, you can choose *Inside/Outside*, meaning that the page margins are for the inner (next to the crease) and outer margins of each page.

⊷ **Note:** Separate values are maintained for Left/Right and Inner/Outer margins. If you change your selection in the Side Margins pulldown, and then change back, the previous values are recalled in the margin fields. This is true even if you save, close, and reopen the document. The Left/Right values are the same as for Single-Sided pages.

The Begin With pulldown is active when **Page Layout** is double-sided. It lets you control whether the first page is a right-hand or left-hand page. If *Any Page* is selected, the combination of the number of the first page and the **Page Layout** setting determine which side the first page falls on. Selecting *Left Page* or *Right Page* instead forces the first page to be to the left or the right, respectively. If the use of *Left Page* or *Right Page* forces a different decision than the **Page Layout** setting would have led to, the number of the first page will be changed so that the *Odd Page Left* or *Odd Page Right* setting will be observed. For example, suppose that the first page is numbered 1 and you select *Odd Page Right*, but you also use *Left Page* to force the first page to the left. The first page will be renumbered as page 2.

In the **Headers/Footers** group, the **Different First Header** and **Different First Footer** buttons allow you to control whether or not the header and footer on the first page of a document differ from those on subsequent pages. If these buttons are on, the header and footer on the first page can be edited without affecting those on subsequent pages.

⊷ **Note:** If you have a multi-page document with a different first header or footer, and you then turn off the **Different First Header/Footer** button, the header or footer from the subsequent pages replaces that on the first page. The header or footer that had been on the first page is lost and cannot be recovered by undoing the change to the **Different First Header/Footer** button.

If the **Bleed** button is on, the headers and footers extend into the side margins of the document's pages.

The Orientation pulldown gives you a choice of *Portrait* or *Landscape*. Portrait orientation means that the height of the page is at least as great as the width. Landscape orientation means that the width is greater than the height. If you make a selection from this pulldown that makes the orientation inconsistent with the page dimensions, the width and height will be exchanged. Conversely, if you change the dimensions, the orientation may be changed to ensure consistency. If both dimensions are the same, you cannot choose *Landscape*.

The Turn Layout pulldown allows you to choose the orientation of the page headers and footers, irrespective of whether the document is portrait or landscape. If you select *Not Turned*, the default, the headers and footers will be in the same orientation as the document: headers at the top, footers at the bottom, and both reading from left to right. If you select *Clockwise*, headers are to the right of the text area and footers are to the left, and both read from top to bottom. If you select *Counterclockwise*, headers are to the left, footers are to the right, and both run from bottom to top. You can use turned layouts to produce pages that are meant to be bound "sideways" but still have page numbers and headers and footers in the usual place. For example, a large landscape-mode table might have a turned layout when included in a portrait-mode document.

◆ **Tip:** If you need to include in a single document pages with different properties, including size and orientation, you must create a book. Within the book, you can create multiple document files. Each document file must contain pages of uniform size and orientation, but the different documents can have varying page properties. The document corresponding to the book as a whole will consist of all the pages of the document files in the book, ordered according to the left-to-right and top-to-bottom positions of the document icons within the book's window.

You can select any desired number of columns with the **Number of Columns** arrows. If you try to use too many columns for the current page width, the document will be treated as a one-column document.

Gutter Width is active when **Number of Columns** is greater than 1. It specifies the horizontal space between columns.

If **Balance Columns** is on, Interleaf 6 attempts to balance and fill out all the columns that are required to accommodate the text of the document. Otherwise, new columns are opened only as preceding columns are packed.

Document Size Properties

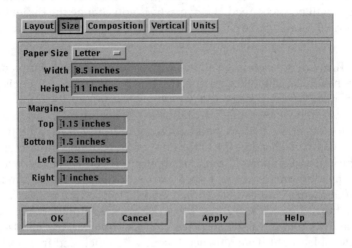

The **Paper Size** pulldown offers a choice of *Letter, Legal, Ledger, A3, A4, A5,* and *B5* paper sizes. If you select one of these, the **Width** and **Height** fields are updated to correspond to the selected size, taking into account whether the current orientation is portrait or landscape. If you enter new values in the **Width** and **Height** fields, then if these values do *not* correspond to one of the listed paper sizes, the **Paper Size** pulldown displays *Custom.* If the entered values *do* correspond to one of the listed paper sizes, the **Paper Size** pulldown displays that size.

The fields in the **Margins** group allow you to specify the top, bottom, and side margins of document pages. The top and bottom margins determine the vertical extent of the headers and footers. If the document is double-sided and **Side Margins** is set to *Inner/Outer* (see page 52), the side margin fields are labeled *Inner* and *Outer.*

◆ **Tip:** If you reduce the top or bottom margins, thereby shrinking headers or footers, some content of the headers or footers may become invisible (obscured) because it extends beyond the new boundary of the header or footer. This can happen to material located near the lower part of either headers or footers. To avoid this, move such material higher when decreasing the top or bottom margins. If material is obscured in this way, you can make it visible again by increasing the margin(s).

Document Composition Properties

```
Layout| Size | Composition | Vertical | Units|

 ☐ Hyphenation
Maximum Consecutive Hyphenated Lines  3        ▭

Rev Bar Placement  Left        ▭
   ☐ Rev Bars Persistent
   ☐ Freeze Autonumbers

          Spacing Between Components  Add        ▭
   Top/Bottom Margins Measured Between  Components ▭

Composition Font System  ileaf ▭

      OK          Cancel          Apply          Help
```

The **Hyphenation** button specifies whether or not hyphenation is permitted. If it is, the Maximum Consecutive Hyphenated Lines pulldown offers a choice of numbers from 1 to 4 or *No Limit*. This determines the number of consecutive lines that can end with a hyphen.

Rev Bar Placement offers a choice of *Left*, *Right*, and *Automatic*. *Left* and *Right* position revision bars to the specified side of the column containing the revised text. *Automatic* positions them in varying ways depending on the number of columns, but always adjacent to the column containing the revision.

Select **Rev Bars Persistent** to ensure that all text entered is flagged with revision bars.

You can select **Freeze Autonumbers** to ensure that autonumbers currently in the document do not lose their token values (visible strings) when other autonumbers are created or deleted.

•◦ **Note:** Using **Freeze Autonumbers** can result in gaps in the autonumber sequence or duplicate autonumber token values.

◆ **Tip:** You can use **Freeze Autonumbers** to cause deliberate gaps in the sequence of autonumber token values. For instance, if an autonumber stream displays values as lower case letters, it is sometimes desirable to skip the letter "l" to avoid confusion with the digit "1." To do this, create all desired autonumbers, and introduce an empty entry for the letter "l." Then, turn on **Freeze Autonumbers** and delete the "l" entry. The sequence will run from "k" to "m." However, if you turn **Freeze Autonumbers** off, entries will be renumbered to make a continuous sequence.

Document Vertical Properties

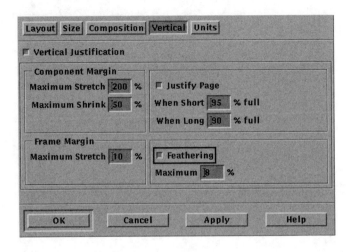

This section of the *Document Properties* dialog box governs vertical justification. This is the insertion of extra space between the top-level objects of a page (or column) so that the contents stretch from top to bottom, rather than ending partway down. To enable vertical justification and activate the fields on this property sheet, you must select **Vertical Justification**.

Vertical justification is performed by increasing or decreasing the space between top-level components or increasing the space above and below frames. Optionally, space may be added between lines within components.

In the **Component Margin** group, the **Maximum Stretch** field is a number from 0 to 400% that defines the amount by which Interleaf 6 can increase component top and bottom margins. The **Maximum Shrink** field is a number from 0 to 100% that defines the amount by which Interleaf 6 can decrease component top and bottom margins.

In the **Frame Margin** group, the **Maximum Stretch** field is a number from 0 to 100% that defines the amount by which Interleaf 6 can increase frame top and bottom margins.

If **Justify Page** is on, Interleaf 6 will attempt to fill out pages to exactly the specified height. The **When Short** field specifies how nearly full a short page (the final page or a page ended by a forced break) must be for vertical justification to take effect. The **When Long** field specifies how nearly full a long page (a page terminated by an unbreakable block) must be for vertical justification to take effect.

Feathering, a number from 0 to 100%, controls the addition of space between lines within components. If it is 0, no space will be added.

The following is a summary of the vertical justification controls:

☐ The **Vertical Justification** button determines whether these features are enabled or disabled.

☐ If **Vertical Justification** is on, the **Justify Page** group determines whether or not Interleaf 6 attempts to vertically justify a given page.

☐ If Interleaf 6 tries to vertically justify a page, the **Component Margin**, **Frame Margin**, and **Feathering** groups determine whether or not the page can be justified, and if so, where additional space will be distributed.

Document Units Properties

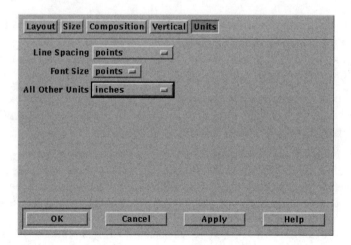

This section of the *Document Properties* dialog box allows you to specify units of measure. There are three pulldowns: one for the **Line Spacing** option in the **Format** section of the *Component Properties* dialog box (see page 31), one for font sizes in any context, and one for all other units. Each pulldown lists all the available units for that category. If you change a unit, the change takes effect immediately, updating any displayed values in open dialog boxes for the current document.

Edit Rulings in table

ACCESS: Document menu bar: Tables→Edit Rulings. . .

FUNCTION: Set properties of table rules

A *Rulings* dialog box is opened:

The *Edit Rulings* menu item on the Document menu bar Tables pull-down toggles to *Close Edit*. Selecting *Close Edit* closes the *Rulings* dialog box. Moving the component bar cursor out of the table also closes the *Rulings* dialog box.

↔ Note: There is no **Apply** function on the *Rulings* dialog box. All changes take effect immediately, and cannot be undone other than by reversing them using this dialog box.

Table rules are selectable segments; you must select a segment in order to operate on it with this dialog box. The upper and lower table rules and left and right table rules are selected as a unit. For example, you cannot select only that part of a left border that is adjacent to one cell. Rules within the table, separating cells vertically or horizontally, are selectable in one-cell segments. All selected rulings blink.

When you open this dialog box, the mouse cursor becomes a rulings cursor. Clicking the left mouse button with the cursor over any rule segment in the table deselects all other segments and selects that segment. Clicking the middle mouse button over a rule segment causes that segment to toggle its selection state without deselecting other segments.

◆ Tip: You can select a hidden (invisible) rule by clicking over its position. The rules will blink visibly as a gray line. Also, you can view invisible table rulings (see page 81).

Within the **Select:** area, six buttons allow you to select rulings rapidly. **All Rows** selects all horizontal rules within the table. **All Columns** selects all vertical rules. **Table Borders** selects the left, right, upper, and lower table borders. These buttons do not deselect any rules that you may have already selected.

➥ **Note:** The horizontal rules between header and footer rows and the rest of the table are considered to be border rules and will be selected by the **Table Borders** button but not by the **All Rows** button.

All Rulings selects all the rules within the table. **Deselect** deselects all rules. **Again** selects all rules that were selected before **Deselect** was pressed.

In the **Visible** group, **Show** makes all selected rules visible and **Hide** makes them invisible. You can view hidden rulings on-screen as gray lines, though they will not print (see page 81).

➥ **Note:** If the **Border Ruling** button of a row property sheet is off (see page 128), the table will not have vertical border rule segments adjacent to that row, regardless of settings made with this dialog box.

In the **Number** group, the **Single** and **Double** buttons control whether a rule is a single or double line.

The **Color** palette allows you to select a color for the rule.

The Weight pulldown brings up a list of points sizes and sample lines from which you may select a weight (thickness) for selected rules. This list also contains a *Numeric...* choice, which opens a dialog box into which you may enter a numeric weight from 0 to 6.125 points.

Edit Tool Bar

ACCESS: Document menu bar: Tools→Edit Tool Bar. . .

FUNCTION: Modify document tool bars

This menu choice allows adding items to or removing items from either the text tool bar or graphics tool bar. The change is made within any document, but affects all documents. An *Edit Tool Bar* dialog box is opened:

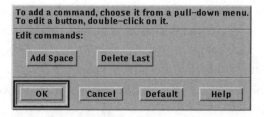

Selecting **Add Space** adds a small horizontal line to the right end of the tool bar. This is used to delineate groups of related tools; it has no function as a tool.

Selecting **Delete Last** removes the right-most object on the tool bar, whether this is a tool or a dash added with **Add Space**.

With this dialog box displayed, you can select any tool for editing by clicking the select mouse button on it. The following dialog box is displayed:

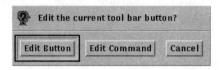

Select **Edit Button** to open a raster image edit window in which you can modify the appearance of the tool.

Select **Edit Command** to change the function of an icon. The following window is opened:

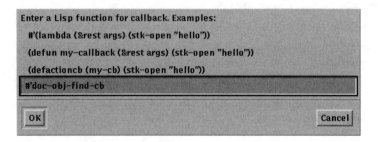

In the text field, you can enter an Interleaf 6 Lisp expression that will be executed when the icon is selected.

Any menu choice available from the document menu bar may be added to a document tool bar. This allows rapid access to it. Only *final* menu selections may be added; selections that bring up additional submenus may not be used in this procedure.

To add a menu choice to a tool bar as a new tool:

1. Make the tool bar you wish to change (text or graphics) be visible.

2. Select Edit→Tool Bar from the document menu bar Edit pulldown, displaying an *Edit Tool Bar* dialog box.

3. Select the document menu bar pulldown menu choice that you wish to add to the tool bar.

A new tool will be added to the right end of the tool bar. Its appearance will be a picture of a wrench, and its Lisp function will correspond to the menu item you selected. The appearance may be modified by selecting the tool while the *Edit Tool Bar* dialog box is visible, and following the procedure described above for modifying an existing tool.

Selecting **Cancel** on the *Edit Tool Bar* dialog box cancels any changes made since the dialog box was opened. Selecting **Default** on the *Edit Tool Bar* dialog box restores the tool bar to its default configuration (as of the installation of Interleaf 6), subject to a confirmation stickup. Selecting **OK** on the *Edit Tool Bar* dialog box closes the dialog box, leaving in effect any changes made while it was open.

Empty cell(s) in table

SELECTION: Yes

ACCESS: Document menu bar: Tables→Empty Cell(s)

FUNCTION: Remove table cell contents

At least one table cell must be selected.

The contents of all selected table cells, other than graphics cells, are discarded.

- **Note:** Graphics cells that contain any content that has been added since the cell was set to use the graphics editor are not affected.

- **Note:** The discarded contents are not placed on the clipboard and cannot be pasted. They can be retrieved with **Undo**.

Exit Interleaf 6

ACCESS: Desktop menu bar: File→Exit
               Document menu bar: File→Exit

FUNCTION: Stop Interleaf 6

This brings up a confirmation dialog box for exiting Interleaf 6, even if the current container is not the desktop. If the user confirms, and no files are open under Interleaf 6, Interleaf 6 terminates execution and all its windows are closed. If there are files open, a dialog box is displayed, allowing the operator to save open files if desired, hold or discard changes, or cancel exiting Interleaf 6.

Expand link

SELECTION: Yes

ACCESS: Desktop menu bar: Tools→Admin→Expand

FUNCTION: Copy a linked container

The selected icon must be a link to a container (directory). The link is replaced by a container of the same class as the link, containing links to all the icons in the original container.

The set of icons accessible in the new container is the same as those accessible via the link. However, the current user is the owner of the new container.

◆ **Tip:** This allows the current user to add and delete icons from the new container, even if the user is not the owner of the original container.

Facing pages visibility

ACCESS: Document menu bar: View→Facing Pages

FUNCTION: Control display of facing pages

This menu item toggles the current document's window between display of a single page and display of facing pages.

File properties

ACCESS: Desktop menu bar: File→File Properties. . .
                Document menu bar: File→File Properties. . .

FUNCTION: Change file properties

A selection is optional if this function is accessed from the document menu bar, and required if accessed from the desktop menu bar. If accessed from the document menu bar, the current document's file properties are displayed.

This dialog box has two pages, selected by the **Interleaf Info** and **File Info** radio buttons. The first button displays a page of information about properties of the icon (file) determined by Interleaf. The second displays a page of information determined by the host file system.

The **Interleaf Info** page:

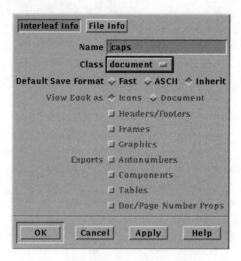

The icon's name is displayed in the field labeled **Name** and can be changed by editing it in this field.

The icon's class is displayed in the **Class** pulldown. Class is a property that specifies the type of file and determines how Interleaf 6 treats it. For example, Interleaf 6 documents, host files, and image files have contents of very different types. Some classes permit their icons to be shifted into compatible classes. For example, a document may be made into a catalogue. This is done by clicking the select button on the **Class** pulldown and selecting the desired class from the resulting pop-up menu.

There are three **Default Save Format** radio buttons: **Fast, ASCII,** and **Inherit,** which apply to documents. **Fast** means save the document in binary format, which opens quickly. **ASCII** means save as Interleaf 6 ASCII markup. **Inherit** causes the save format (**Fast** or **ASCII**) to be determined by the document's container.

The **View Book as** line is active only for books. When you select and open a book icon, if the **Icons** radio button is on, a container window opens displaying the contents of the book as icons. If the **Document** radio button is on, the first document within the book is opened in a document window, and you can work with the document contents of the book without having to see the container window or file icons.

The various **Exports** buttons control catalog export properties. They can only be selected if the icon's class is catalog.

The **File Info** page (Sun/OS example):

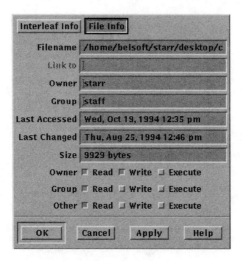

The path to the icon is displayed in the **Filename** field, which is read-only.

If the icon is a link to another file, the path of the file linked to is displayed in the **Link to** field. This field may be edited, which changes the target of the link.

➤ **Note:** If the entered path is invalid or points to a file that is incompatible with the class of the selected icon, the link will not operate correctly.

The **Owner** and **Group** fields display operating system-specific properties of the file and may be edited.

The **Owner, Group,** and **Other** buttons display operating system-specific access permissions of the file and may be toggled to change these properties.

The **Last Accessed**, **Last Changed**, and **Size** fields display operating system-specific information about the file and are read-only.

Find and change text

ACCESS: 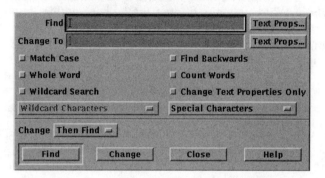 Document menu bar: Edit→Find/Change...
Text tool bar

FUNCTION: Search for and replace document text

A *Find & Change* dialog box is opened:

If there is a text selection, it will be the initial content of the **Find** field. You can click in this field and enter or modify its contents. When you select **Find**, the next occurrence in the current document of the text in the **Find** field will be found and highlighted. Searches proceed forward from the text cursor, unless the **Find Backwards** button is selected.

The Change pulldown lets you change individual or multiple occurrences of the text in the **Find** field. If you select the **Find** button, the next occurrence is found and highlighted. The Change pulldown then offers the following choices:

Change & Find: The highlighted occurrence of the **Find** text is replaced by the contents of the **Change to** field, and Interleaf 6 immediately finds and highlights the next occurrence.

Single: The highlighted occurrence of the **Find** text is replaced by the contents of the **Change to** field.

To End: All occurrences of the **Find** text from the current selection or text cursor position to the end of the document are replaced by the contents of the **Change to** field.

◆ **Tip:** You can "replace to beginning" by selecting **Find Backwards** and using the **To End** operation.

All: All occurrences of the **Find** text in the current document are replaced by the contents of the **Change to** field.

If there is *no* text highlighted as a result of a search, you can use only the **To End** and **All** choices on the Change pulldown.

Leaving the **Change to** field empty and executing a replacement deletes the found text.

If **Match Case** is selected, the search will only find occurrences in the text that match the **Find** field with respect to case; otherwise, capital and lowercase versions of the same letter are considered to match.

If **Whole Word** is selected, the search will not find substrings within words. For example, suppose the **Find** field contains "other." Selecting **Whole Word** prevents finding the "other" within "mother" or "brother." *This option is not available if* **Find Backwards** *is selected.*

If **Count Words** is selected, the number of occurrences of the **Find** text in the current document is displayed. If **Whole Word** is also selected, only occurrences that are whole words are counted. *This option is not available if* **Find Backwards** *is selected.*

Wildcard Search allows you to input more complex specifications of strings to find. Instead of matching the **Find** string exactly, you can match various combinations of characters. When **Wildcard Search** is selected, the Wildcard Characters pulldown lists the available options, and provides a shortcut to entering them in the **Find** field. *This option is not available if* **Find Backwards** *is selected.*

The Special Characters pulldown allows you to enter special characters such as tab and hard return in the **Find** and **Change to** fields. These characters are represented as "escape sequences" such as "\r" for hard return. You can type them in directly; the pulldown provides a convenient list and a shortcut to entry.

You can specify text properties for either searching or replacing. Selecting the **Text Props...** button adjacent to the **Find** or the **Change to** field opens a *Find Properties* dialog box or a *Change Properties* dialog box, respectively. These dialog boxes display the same fields:

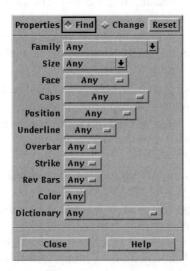

The *Find Properties* dialog box lets you specify text properties that must be matched when searching for an occurrence of the **Find** text. *Any* (the default) means that any value will match. The *Change Properties* dialog box lets you specify text properties that will be applied to the **Change to** text when a replacement is done. *As Found* (the default) means that the property will take its value from the occurrence of the **Find** text. These dialog boxes are not accessible if **Wildcard Search** or **Find Backwards** are selected. The *Change Properties* dialog box is not accessible if **Count Words** is selected.

◆ **Tip:** You can search for text properties without entering any **Find** text. For example, by specifying **Face** as *Bold*, you can find any boldface text.

If **Change Text Properties Only** is selected, the **Change to** field becomes inaccessible and the two **Text Props...** buttons can be selected. Any replacement operation changes the text properties of the found text to those specified in the *Change Properties* dialog box.

◆ **Tip:** You can enter special character sequences in the **Find** and **Replace** fields to match extended characters. To do so, open a character palette (see page 43). Find the character in question by selecting the font and looking at the palette pages for that font. Click the select button once on the character. A message will appear at the bottom of the character palette giving the hexadecimal character code for that character. You can represent that character in the **Find** and **Replace** fields by typing this sequence: backslash, x, the hexadecimal code, backslash. For example, if you click on lower-case o with an umlaut on the second Swiss page, the message "Character code is F6" will appear. You can represent this character for searching and replacing with the string " \xF6\."

Find object in document

ACCESS: 　Document menu bar: Edit→Find Object
　　　　　Text tool bar

FUNCTION:　Find an object within a document

This command allows you to find objects other than text within the current document. A *Find Object* dialog box is opened:

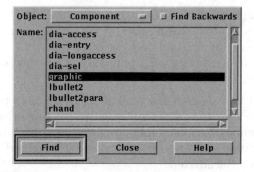

The Object pulldown lists types of objects that you can search for, and displays the type that will currently be searched for if you select **Find**. The **Name:** list displays the names available for the selected object type. Specifying a name finds only objects of that name (master). Specifying *(Any)* finds any object of that type.

◆ **Tip:** If there is a *Find Object* dialog box open for the current document, you can modify the **Object** and **Name:** settings. If there is *not* a *Find Object* dialog box open for the current document, and you open one, if there is any object other than simple text selected, the selection determines the settings of **Object** and **Name:**. It may be convenient to close the dialog box and reopen it to take advantage of this. If there is no selection, or only simple text is selected, the current top-level component determines the initial settings.

Objects are searched for, beginning with the current text cursor position. Searches move forward within the document, unless **Find Backwards** is selected.

Font size in table cells

SELECTION: Yes

ACCESS: Document menu bar: Tables→Fonts

FUNCTION: Change font size of table cells

At least one table cell must be selected.

This menu choice offers a choice of two submenu items, *Larger* and *Smaller*. Selecting either one increases or reduces the font sizes of text in the selected cells, including microdocument text within graphics cells. Text within inline components is not affected.

Fonts in document text

ACCESS: Document text area menu

FUNCTION: Change font in document text

This menu choice allows you to change either the current font (for new typing) or the font of existing text. If you execute these commands with a text selection, the font of the selected text will change. If there is no selection, the change will apply only to new text entered at the point at which you make the change.

➥ **Note:** If the selection spans all or parts of nested inline components, the change will not apply within the nested inlines, except nested inlines that inherit font properties (see page 26). If the selection is within an inline, selected text at the top level of that inline will always be affected.

A submenu of five choices opens:

Copy: The font at the current text position is copied (this copy is internal to Interleaf 6 and does not use the clipboard, and does not affect the next paste of text). If there is a text selection, the font at the beginning of the selection is copied.

Paste: The font copied by the preceding Fonts→Copy operation is pasted at the current text location. If there is a text selection, the selection is converted to the pasted font (see the note above about nested inlines). This paste does not use the clipboard and is not affected by clipboard cut/copy/paste operations.

Size: This brings up a submenu of three choices. You can select **Smaller** or **Larger** to change the size of the current font or selection. If there is a selection and it contains several font sizes, each part of the selection is reduced or enlarged by one available font size. Or, you can select **Numeric**, to open this dialog box:

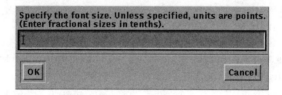

You can enter a size from 2 to 200 points.

◆ **Tip:** This allows you to use sizes outside the usual range for the font.

Bold: This brings up a submenu of three choices. You can selected *Off* or *On* to turn boldface off or on. Or, select *Toggle* to change lightface text to boldface and vice versa.

Italic: This brings up a submenu of three choices. You can selected *Off* or *On* to turn italic off or on. Or, select *Toggle* to change roman text to italic and vice versa.

Frame properties

SELECTION: Yes

ACCESS: Document menu bar: Properties→Frame. . .
              Document text menu

FUNCTION: Change properties of frame

A *Frame Properties* dialog box is opened. This dialog box has three pages, selected via the **Layout**, **Content**, and **Anchor** radio buttons.

Frame Layout Properties

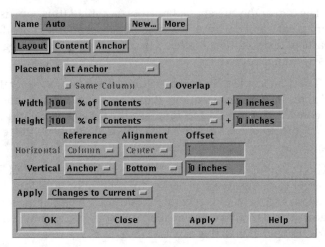

The Placement pulldown lists the frame placement types: *At Anchor,*
Following Anchor, Top, Following Text, Bottom, Overlay, and *Underlay.*
The **Placement** property determines which of the other fields and buttons in this section of the dialog box are applicable. Those that are not
appropriate for the selected Placement are not selectable.

If Placement is *Following Anchor, Top, Following Text,* or *Bottom,* the
Same Column button specifies whether or not the frame is supposed
to appear in the same column as its anchor. If Placement is *At Anchor,*
the **Overlap** button determines whether or not the frame is allowed to
overlap text; if this button is off, the frame displaces text.

◆ **Tip:** An **At Anchor** frame with **Overlap** on can be clipped by text,
   that is, part of the frame may be obscured by text and not visible.
   To use a frame to create a screen or other graphic as a background
   to text, set **Placement** to **Underlay**.

The **Width** and **Height** groups allow you to specify the dimensions of
the frame. The pulldown menus in these sections list choices of *Contents* (meaning that the frame's width or height is made just large
enough to accommodate its contents), *Fixed* (meaning that you can alter the dimension by keying in a new value), or various combinations
of page dimensions, column width, page gutter, and page margins.
These combinations allow you to fit the frame to the page or column
layout rather than to its contents. In all cases except *Fixed* size, you can
apply a percent multiplier and a constant additive modifier to the dimension.

With the **Alignment** group, you specify how the frame is to be positioned either in relation to its anchor or in relation to the page layout.

Horizontal and vertical positions are specified separately and may be modified by fixed numeric offsets. For horizontal positions, positive offsets indicate a shift to the right, and negative offsets shift to the left. For vertical positions, positive offsets indicate a downward shift, and negative offsets shift toward the top of the page.

Frame Content Properties

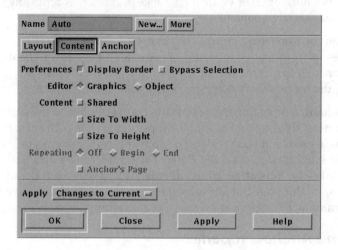

Display Border determines whether or not the frame will be surrounded by a gray border when it is open for editing its contents. If **Bypass Selection** is on, clicking the select mouse button on the frame does not select the frame but opens it immediately.

The **Editor** radio buttons enable you to select which of two editors is started when you open the frame for editing. The graphics editor is appropriate for vector graphics. The object editor is appropriate for raster images (bitmap graphics), microdocuments, charts, and equations.

In the **Content** group, the **Shared** button determines whether or not the frame is shared content (all instances of this frame name have the same content).

Size To Width and **Size To Height** adjust the dimensions of the frame's contents to match its current size. If these buttons are on, then whenever you close the frame, the contents will be sized to fit. Also, changing the frame's size property causes the contents to resize, even if the frame is closed.

→ **Note:** If you change the size of objects in the frame by turning on the properties **Size To Width** or **Size To Height**, turning the properties off will not undo the change to the frame's contents.

• **Note:** The **Size To Width** and **Size To Height** buttons do not affect microdocuments or text strings.

A repeating frame is one that is duplicated on every page within a consecutive range of pages. Only frames with Placement of *Top, Bottom, Following Text, Overlay,* or *Underlay* may be designated as repeating (see page 70). An overlay or underlay frame cannot be a repeating frame if it has a horizontal or vertical reference of *Anchor.* A repeating frame must have shared content.

Within the **Repeating** group, **Off** causes a frame to not repeat. **Begin** causes the frame to be repeating. If **Anchor's Page** is on, the first appearance of the frame will be on the same page as the anchor. Otherwise, the frame will first appear on the page following the anchor.

By default, a repeating frame appears on every page to the end of the document. If you want to end its appearance sooner than that, go to the page on which you want its last appearance. Create a new instance of the same master, open the *Frame Properties* dialog box, and select **End** from the **Repeating** group. If **Anchor's Page** is on, the frame will appear on this page but not subsequent pages. If **Anchor's Page** is off, the frame will last appear on the page preceding the anchor.

Frame Anchor Properties

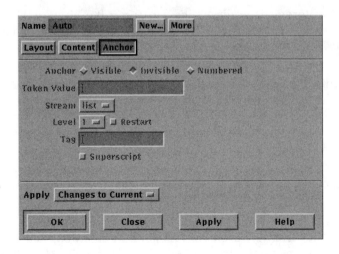

The key to the **Anchor** properties is the three radio buttons: **Visible** causes the frame's anchor to be visible on the screen (it does not affect the appearance of the document when printed). **Invisible** makes the anchor invisible on the screen (it does not displace any other object when invisible). **Numbered** causes the anchor to be associated with an autonumber token, whose value is visible both on screen and in printed output as the frame's anchor.

If **Numbered** is on, the remaining fields in this section of the dialog box define the autonumber's properties. **Token Value** is a read-only display of the anchor's autonumber token value. The Stream pulldown lists available autonumber streams. **Level** lists the levels defined for the selected stream. **Restart**, if on, specifies that the stream should restart with its initial token value. **Tag** is an autonumber tag that can be used to create an autonumber reference to the frame. **Superscript** controls whether or not the visible autonumber will be superscript text.

Frames with numbered anchors are useful for creating footnotes (as exemplified in the template documents supplied with Interleaf 6). Create a frame at the point in the text where you want the footnote indicator to appear. Adjust the frame's properties to position it where you want your footnote to be visible, typically at the bottom of the page. Put the footnote text in the frame as a microdocument. Within the microdocument, create a reference to an autonumber, and enter a tag matching the contents of the **Tag** field from the frame's anchor properties. The reference will visibly link the footnote to the numbered anchor.

Frame Settings

ACCESS: Document menu bar: Change➔Frame Settings

FUNCTION: Access dialog boxes for graphics settings

This menu selection provides direct access, through a submenu of four choices, to four of the dialog boxes accessible through the graphics editing palette: *Grid* (see page 154), *Fill/Edge* (see page 152), *Text Defaults* (see page 159), and *Animation* (see page 155).

GoTo container

ACCESS: Desktop menu bar: GoTo pulldown

FUNCTION: Display specified directory (container)

This pulldown allows you to select a file system directory to display in the current window.

If the directory you select is already displayed in a window, that window is opened and brought to the front. Otherwise, the selected directory's contents are displayed in the current window.

Selections that choose a directory are **Desktop** (the user's desktop), **System6** (the System6 cabinet), **.. (Up a Level)** (the parent of the directory currently displayed), and history list entries (container directory names) that have been recently accessed in the current Interleaf 6 session. Selecting *Add Directory to List* adds the current container to the upper part of the list.

If you select **Pathname**, a *GoTo Pathname* dialog box opens:

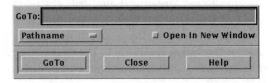

You can select *Desktop* or *Bulletin Board* on the pulldown. Or, you can select *Pathname*, enter a directory path in the **Go To:** field, and select **Go To** to open the specified directory. If **Open In New Window** is on, the directory is opened in a new window; otherwise, it replaces the current directory in the current window.

Graphics show or hide

ACCESS: Document menu bar: View→Pulldown

FUNCTION: Control display of frames and frame contents

Three entries on the document menu bar View pulldown let you control the display of graphics. By turning off display that you do not need while working on text, you can obtain faster performance and sometimes a clearer view of the text.

Two entries, *Overlay Frames* and *Underlay Frames*, control whether or not these kinds of frames are displayed at all. Since neither affects pagination, all other elements of your document will have the same positions in either case.

The *Graphics* selection determines whether other kinds of frames will be displayed in full or simply as empty boxes of the correct size.

Hyphen in document content

ACCESS: Document menu bar: Edit→Hyphen

FUNCTION: Display and modify hyphenation points

This menu choice allows display and modification of hyphenation points. It uses only the first word of the text selection, or the word containing the text caret if there is no selection. It brings up a submenu of these choices: *Show, Set, Reset,* and *Clear.*

Show	This menu item displays the hyphenation points of the first word of the text selection, or the word containing the text caret if there is no selection, on the document's message line. If there is no dictionary entry for the word, a message to this effect is added.
Set	A hyphenation point is established at the position of the text caret. This means that the word can be broken (hyphenated) at that point.
Reset	The hyphenation points of all words in the text selection are reset as specified by the dictionary (or by algorithm if there is no dictionary entry). Hyphenation points added with *Set* are discarded. Hyphenation points removed with *Clear* are made effective again, except those initially specified with *Set*. The hyphenation points of a word are reset if any part of the word is selected.
Clear	If there is text selected, all hyphenation points in words in the text selection are removed. If there is no text selected but there is a hyphenation point at the position of the text caret, that hyphenation point is removed.

Import into document

ACCESS: Document menu bar: File→Import

FUNCTION: Import a file (icon) into document content

A *File Selection* dialog box is opened (see page 116). This dialog box has an **Import** button that imports the selected icon.

The contents of a separate icon are imported into the current document. The result of this depends on the type of the other icon. For example, if the other icon is an Interleaf document, its entire contents as a series of top-level components are inserted into the current document. If the other icon is an ASCII text file, it is inserted as a series of default components. If the other icon is an Interleaf image, it is inserted as a frame containing the image.

Import/Export files

SELECTION: Yes

ACCESS: Desktop menu bar: File→Import/Export. . .

FUNCTION: Convert a document or file to a different format

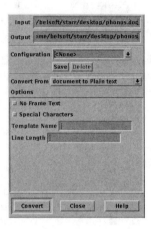

This dialog box allows "filtering" (converting) the selected icon(s) from one format to another. For example, an Interleaf document may be converted to a Microsoft Word document, or a TIFF image may be converted to an Interleaf image.

The text field labeled **Input** is the path of the next icon to be converted. It is prefilled with the path of the most recently selected icon.

◆   **Tip:** This path cannot be edited, but it can be changed simply by selecting another icon, even if it is in a different window.

The text field labeled **Output** is the path for the output. The default is based on the **Input** path.

The **Convert From** pulldown displays the currently selected conversion. Clicking the select button on the down arrow at the right side of this window displays a list of all available methods. Any method listed may be selected with the mouse:

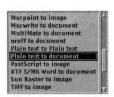

The box labeled **Options** may contain buttons or text fields, or both, specific to the conversion method specified in the **Convert From** sub-window.

The **Configuration** pulldown may contain the name of a file in which the options in the **Options** box may be saved. This name may be edited by clicking the select button on this field. Selecting the down arrow at the right side of this pulldown displays a list of all available configuration files:

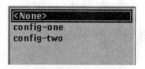

Any displayed file may be used by selecting it with the mouse, causing the options specified in the configuration file to be displayed in the **Options** window and also setting the conversion method in the **Convert From** field to be the one specified in the conversion file.

↝ **Note:** Selecting a conversion file specifies both conversion method and options.

Selecting the **Save** button beneath the **Configuration** field saves a new configuration file or overwrites an existing one. Selecting the **Delete** button beneath the **Configuration** field deletes the configuration file currently specified.

Selecting the **Convert** button at the bottom of the *Import/Export* dialog box executes the conversion.

If a configuration file is saved, its name is added to the desktop menu bar Tools→Selection→Filter→menu. Selecting an icon and then executing this menu choice automatically executes the import/export operation specified by the configuration file. This provides a fast approach to export/import operations, skipping the dialog box altogether.

Index within book

SELECTION: Yes

ACCESS: Desktop menu bar: Book pulldown

FUNCTION: Create an index document for a book

With this menu selection, you can create one or more index documents for the current book. Only selected documents or sub-books will be included in the index.

A tear-off sub-menu will open, offering you a choice of *Normal* or *Master*. The difference is that a normal index contains only page number references, whereas a Master index lists the names of the selected documents or sub-books in addition to page numbers.

The index documents created appear within the current book. Their names are determined by the index token properties in the documents selected for indexing (see page 78).

◆ **Tip:** It is recommended that you execute a Book→Sync before generating an index, to ensure that all information is up-to-date.

Index token edit properties

SELECTION: Yes

ACCESS: Desktop menu bar Create pulldown
Desktop menu bar Edit pulldown
Document text menu

FUNCTION: Modify (or create) index entry

This dialog box allows modification of all the properties of an index token.

An *Index Token Properties* dialog box is opened when you create a new index token, or when you select an index token and edit its properties. It allows modification of all the properties of an index token.

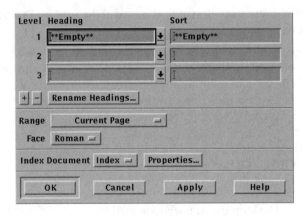

The fields under **Heading** are the headings that will be printed for this entry in the index. Under **Sort** are the sort keys that will be used to put index entries in order. The sort keys are identical to the headings by default, but may be modified.

When you create a new index token, the headings and sort fields are initialized to **Empty** unless there is a text selection, in which case the selection is the initial content of the Level 1 fields.

The pulldown menu to the right of the first-level heading field displays a list of all the first-level index headings in the current document. You can duplicate an existing heading in the current dialog box by selecting it on the pulldown menu. The pulldown menu to the right of the second-level heading field lists all second-level headings that are in the current document in index tokens that have the same first-level heading as that displayed in the dialog box. This is carried through all the lower levels. This provides a convenient way of creating multiple index entries that differ only in the lower levels. You can also drag and drop text between the different fields.

◆ **Tip:** You can use characters that you cannot type into an index field by entering numeric markup. First, obtain the hexadecimal code for the character as described for the **Find in Document Text** command (see page 67). Then, at the point in the index text where you want the character to appear, type this sequence: left angle bracket, pound sign, the hexadecimal code, right angle bracket. For example, if you want to use an opening double quote, you will find that the hexadecimal code is 7F. You can use this in an index by typing "<#7F>."

The + button adds heading/sort fields to this dialog box, to a limit of six. The - button reduces the number of fields, but will only remove empty fields.

The **Rename Headings** button opens a *Rename Index Headings* dialog box:

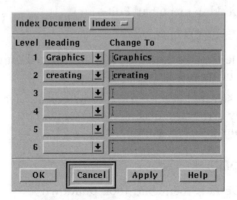

You can select any first-level heading in the current document from the pulldown menu to the right of the first heading field. By entering a new value in the first **Change To** field and selecting **Apply,** you can cause all index tokens in the current document that have the selected first-level heading to be changed so that they have the heading in the **Change To** field. Similarly, you can select any existing combination of headings at more than one level, and apply a change to any or all of them in a single operation.

Join cells in table

SELECTION: Yes

ACCESS: Document menu bar: Tables→Join Cells

FUNCTION: Create or extend a straddle in a table by joining cells

There must be cells in more than one column or more than one row selected. If cells in the same row are selected, they are joined to create a horizontal straddle. If cells in the same column are selected, they are joined to create a vertical straddle.

Line up icons

SELECTION: Yes

ACCESS: Desktop menu bar: View→Line Up Icons

FUNCTION: Line up icons within a container

The selected icons are repositioned to form orderly rows within the current container's window.

Link icon

ACCESS: Desktop menu bar: Edit→Link

FUNCTION: Create file links

Links are made to the selected icon(s) and placed on the clipboard. They can then be pasted in the desired container.

If no icons are selected in the current container, a *NoName* link icon is created directly in the current container. You can rename this icon and enter a valid link path (see page 62).

List directory

ACCESS: Desktop menu bar: Tools pulldown

FUNCTION: List a file system directory

A stayup window displays a host file system directory listing.

If icons are selected in the current window, the files corresponding to those icons are listed. Otherwise, the contents of the directory corresponding to the current window are listed. If a selected icon is a link to a container, the path linked to is displayed, not the contents of the container linked to.

◆ **Tip:** Listing with no selection displays all files in the directory. Listing with a selection does not display Interleaf 6 auxiliary files that may be associated with the selected icons. If you simply want a list with one entry per icon, it is more convenient to select all icons in which you are interested.

Markers in document

SELECTION: Optional

ACCESS: Document menu bar: View→Markers

FUNCTION: Hide or show markers in document content

A *View Markers* dialog box is opened:

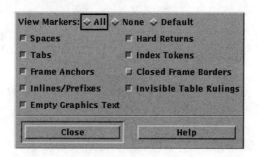

The operator can specify whether each type of in-document marker is to be visible or hidden. **All** displays all markers. **None** hides all markers. **Default** displays all except **Spaces**, **Closed Frame Borders**, and **Invisible Table Rulings**. Turning on **Closed Frame Borders** causes a wavy gray border to appear around all frames (including headers and footers) that are not open. This is a useful way to see the extent of a frame whose visible contents may not completely fill it. Turning on **Invisible Table Rulings** causes hidden table rulings (see page 58) to be visible on-screen as gray lines.

Microdocument properties

ACCESS: Document menu bar: Properties→Microdocument

FUNCTION: Modify properties of microdocuments

A microdocument must be open for this dialog box to be used.

A microdocument is analogous to a miniature document within a frame. Like a document, it can contain top-level components and in-lines, can be multi-column, and has properties that control composition. Unlike a document, a microdocument cannot contain frames or tables.

A *Microdocument Properties* dialog box is opened. This dialog box has three pages.

Microdocument Layout Properties

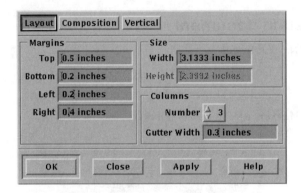

The **Margins** fields specify an area around the borders of the microdocument that must be left free of text, similar to the page margins of a document.

If the microdocument is fixed-width, you can change the width by entering a new value in the **Width** field.

The **Columns** up/down arrow field specifies the number of columns (up to 99) for composing text within the microdocument. **Gutter Width** specifies the distance between columns. If the specified number of columns and gutter width would exceed the width of the microdocument, the microdocument will be composed in one column.

Microdocument Composition Properties

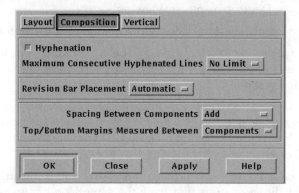

If **Hyphenation** is off, there will be no hyphenation within the microdocument.   Otherwise, the **Maximum Consecutive Hyphenated Lines** pulldown determines the number of consecutive lines that may end in a hyphen. It can specify *No Limit* or a number from one to four.

Revision bars are always placed adjacent to the column containing the text with the Rev Bars property. If **Revision Bar Placement** is *Automatic*, revision bars will always be placed to the left of the text if the number of columns is one. If number of columns is greater than one, revision bars will be placed to the right of the right–most column and to the left of all other columns. If **Revision Bar Placement** is *Left* or *Right*, revision bars will always be placed to the specified side of each column.

Microdocument Vertical Properties

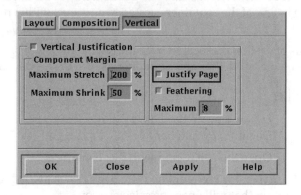

These fields have the same meanings as fields with the same name on the *Document Properties* dialog box (see page 56).

Names of icons

ACCESS: Desktop menu bar View pulldown

FUNCTION: Label desktop icons with icon names or file system names

This menu selection toggles between labeling desktop icons with their icon names and labeling them with the corresponding filenames from the host file system.

The *File Names* selection causes host filenames to be displayed. The *Desktop Names* selection causes the user-assigned icon names to be displayed. When either selection is chosen, it is replaced on the menu by the other one.

◆ **Tip:** Labeling icons with filenames allows you to distinguish between different icons that have the same icon name, as all filenames are made unique. It also allows you to enter filename extensions that assign files to the correct classes, for example, ".rtf" for an RTF word processing file.

New icon

ACCESS: Desktop menu bar: File→New→(submenu)
     Document menu bar: File→New→(submenu)

FUNCTION: Create a new icon (file)

A submenu listing all the icons in the System6 Create cabinet by icon name is displayed. If a choice is made from this submenu, the corresponding icon will be copied from the Create cabinet and the copy will be pasted in the current container.

If the Create cabinet contains any containers, the contents of these containers will be displayed as cascading submenus. You can select any file (icon) in any of the containers nested to any level within the Create cabinet.

When this operation is executed from the document menu bar, the new icon will be placed in the same container as the current document.

Open file

ACCESS: Desktop menu bar: File→Open
     Document menu bar File→Open

FUNCTION: Open an icon (document, file, container)

A *File Selection* dialog box is opened (see page 116). This dialog box has an **Open** button that will open the selected icon.

↔ **Note:** Interleaf 6 for Windows follows Windows conventions for the user interface to opening files.

Page Number Stream properties

ACCESS: Document menu bar: Properties→Page Number Streams

FUNCTION: Define and modify page number streams

A *Page Number Streams* dialog box is opened:

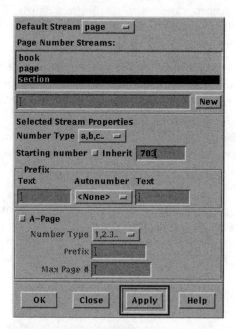

A page number stream defines a numbering sequence for pages. You may use as many streams as you like within a given document or book. This enables you to use one series of numbers for the foreword, another for the body, etc. You may also use several streams on a given page, so that, for example, each page may be separately numbered starting from one within its chapter, within its section, and within the document as a whole. Page number streams may be exported from catalogs.

When you wish to display a page number in a document, create a page number reference (see page 45). The **List** pulldown on the *Create* dialog box allows you to choose a stream. The stream you choose will define the format of the composed page number.

When you create a reference to an autonumber (see page 46), and the **Reference is** field on the *Autonumber Reference* dialog box is *Autonumber Page Location*, the reference is a page number reference. The **Page Stream** pulldown on the dialog box lets you choose the stream to use.

On the *Page Number Streams* dialog box, the **Default Stream** pull-down identifies the default stream to use when creating a page number reference or autonumber.

The **Page Number Streams** list shows all currently defined page number streams. To change the properties of a stream, highlight the stream, select the desired property settings, and press **Apply**. To create a new stream, enter its name in the field to the left of the **New** button, and press the **New** button.

◆ **Tip:** A new page number stream is initialized with the default properties, not the settings on the dialog box. To use different properties, you must first create the stream, then select it and change its properties.

The **Number Type** pulldown lets you select Arabic numerals, upper or lower case roman numerals, or upper or lower case letters to format the page number value. If you use letters, the sequence counts from A to Z, then from AA to AZ, from BA to BZ, and so on.

On the **Starting number** line, if **Inherit** is on, the first page in this document file is numbered to follow the last page of the previous document in the book, if any, or with 1 if none. If **Inherit** is off, the numeric field to the right determines the number of the first page in this document file.

The **Prefix** section specifies an optional prefix for each formatted page number in the stream. With the **Autonumber** pulldown, you can choose <*None*>, for no autonumber, or any defined autonumber stream. If you chose a stream, the current autonumber value will be included in each formatted page number. This allows you to include such information as chapter or section numbers in page numbers. The two **Text** fields specify text which will appear before and after the autonumber (or consecutively, if there is no autonumber stream).

For example, suppose that the selected autonumber stream is for numbering chapters, currently has the value 3, and uses upper case roman numerals. Suppose also that the current page number in the selected page number stream is 27, that the stream uses Arabic numbers, and the the two **Text** fields contain "Chapter " and ", page ." A formatted page number in this stream would be: "Chapter III, page 27."

The **A–Page** section defines page numbering properties for A–Page splitting (see page 17). The Number Type pulldown has the same options as in the **Selected Stream Properties** section. The **Prefix** field can contain an optional text prefix that immediately precedes A–Page numbers. The **Max Page #** field may contain a number that determines the maximum page number that this stream can reach before A–Page numbering begins, even if you do not do an A-Page split. Use a value of zero to specify no maximum.

Paste icon

SELECTION: **No**

ACCESS: Desktop menu bar: Edit→Paste
               Desktop pulldown

FUNCTION: Paste icon into container window

The current clipboard selection, if any, is placed in the current container.

Paste in document text area

ACCESS: Document menu bar: Edit→Paste
               Component bar menu
               Document text menu
               ⌐ Text tool bar

FUNCTION: Paste into document content

The current clipboard selection, if any, is pasted into the current document at the position of the text cursor. The selection remains on the clipboard and can be pasted repeatedly.

•◦ **Note:** If there is a text selection, and you paste into the text area, the selected material is deleted and replaced by the pasted material. The only way to recover the deleted material is by undoing the paste.

Preferences of individual user

ACCESS: Desktop menu bar: Tools→Preferences
               Document menu bar: Tools→Preferences

FUNCTION: Configure Interleaf 6 options

A *Preferences* dialog box is opened. This dialog box presents options on nine pages: Desktop, File, Keyboard, Document, View, Graphics, Tables, General, and Templates. Choose a page by selecting a radio button on the left side of the dialog box. Each category is discussed below, beneath the label of the corresponding radio button.

Desktop Preferences

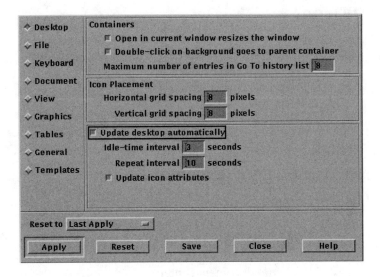

Open in current window resizes the window: If this button is se-lected, executing Open→ In This Window resizes the current window to fit the container being opened.

Double-click on background goes to parent container: If you turn on this button and the **Select** button is double-clicked on the background of a container, the container's parent container (the directory in which the container is a subdirectory) is displayed in either the current win-dow or a separate window.

Maximum number of entries in Go To history list: This numeric field specifies the maximum number of directories that will be maintained on the desktop menu bar GoTo pulldown for quick access.

Icon placement: These two fields determine the spacing of the grid on which desktop icons are aligned. The smaller the values, the more closely icons will be packed.

Update desktop automatically: These fields determine the update in-tervals. To do an update, Interleaf 6 examines the host file system di-rectory corresponding to a desktop container for new files that have no icons and existing icons whose underlying files have been deleted. The desktop container's contents (icons) are adjusted.

☐ **Idle-time interval**: The time the operator must be idle (not use the user interface) for Interleaf 6 to do an update.

☐ **Repeat interval**: The minimum time between updates.

☐ **Update icon attributes**: If this button is on, icon attributes will be included in updates.

File Preferences

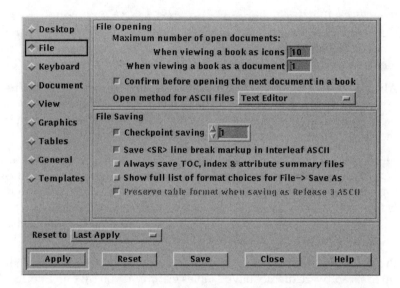

Maximum number of open documents: These fields specify the maximum number of documents that can be open within a single book. If a document is opened beyond the maximum, one of the other open ones is closed. One of the two fields takes effect, depending on whether the book is viewed as icons or as a document (see page 63).

Confirm before opening the next document in a book: With this button on, the operator will be asked to confirm or cancel when paging past the first or last page of a document in a book would cause the next or previous document to be opened.

Open method for ASCII files: You have three choices when opening a host file whose name does not have an extension specifying an Interleaf 6 file type:

▣ **Text Editor**: Host files are opened as straight ASCII files.

▣ **Document**: Host files are opened as Interleaf documents.

▣ **Choose when opening**: The operator is asked to choose one of the above two options each time a host file is opened.

Checkpoint saving: If this option is on, open documents that have changes are periodically saved as checkpoint versions. The frequency of these checkpoints is specified by the associated up and down arrows. The higher the number, the more frequent the saving; 25 is a recommended number to start with.

Save <SR> line break markup in Interleaf ASCII: If this button is selected, the positions of soft returns (line breaks created by Interleaf 6 when composing text) is denoted by "<SR>" when an Interleaf 6 document is saved in ASCII format.

Always save TOC, index & attribute summary files: If you turn this option on, the auxiliary files containing table of contents, attribute, and index information are maintained when you save a document, even if the document is not within a book.

Show full list of format choices for File→Save As: If this button is selected, the *File Save* dialog box displays all available formats for saving a document. The formats fast, ASCII, and Release 5 ASCII (Interleaf 5) are always listed. This button controls the listing of the additional formats: Release 5J ASCII (Interleaf 5 for Japanese), Release 5C ASCII (Interleaf 5.4), Release 4 ASCII (TPS 4), and Release 3 ASCII.

Preserve table format when saving as Release 3 ASCII: Release 3 of Interleaf software did not have a tables feature. If you save an Interleaf 6 document as Release 3 ASCII, and this option is selected, frames are used to approximate the structures of tables. If this option is off, tables will be discarded if you save as Release 3 ASCII. This option is only used if the option **Show full list of format choices for File→Save As**, above, is on, because otherwise the choice to save as Release 3 ASCII is not available.

Keyboard Preferences

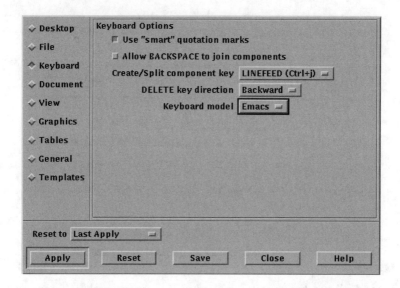

Use "smart" quotation marks: If this feature is on, Interleaf 6 tries to figure out from the current text entry context whether a double quote should be an opening double quote (") or a closing double quote ("). You can key a double quote, type some quoted text, and key another double quote. The first double quote will be an opening double quote; the second, a closing double quote. If this option is off, you must press the ESC key before keying a double quote to obtain an opening double quote.

Allow BACKSPACE to join components: If you select this option, then when the text cursor is at the beginning of a top-level component, pressing the backspace key joins that component with the preceding component.

Create/Split component key: This pulldown has two entries, **LINE-FEED (Ctrl+j)** and **RETURN**. It determines whether the function of creating and splitting components is bound to the linefeed key (equivalent to Control-J) or the return key.

DELETE key direction: This menu has two choices, which determine whether striking the Delete key deletes the character immediately before the text insertion point (*Backward*) or immediately after it (*Forward*).

Keyboard model: This allows you to choose between Emacs and PC key bindings, affecting the keystroke shortcuts to various operations.

Document Preferences

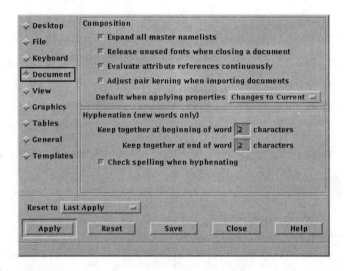

Expand all master namelists: Names of masters (such as frame and component masters) and streams may contain colons. If they do, Interleaf 6 views such names as hierarchies, with the "root" being the part up to the colon and the "branch" the part after it. When these names are displayed in lists, there are two modes for display of these hierarchies. If the **Expand all master namelists** option is on, each root is displayed with a minus sign as a suffix, and all branches of names beginning with that root are displayed, indented, beneath it. If this option is off, each root is displayed with a plus sign as a suffix, and the branches are not displayed at all, making a shorter list. In either case, you can toggle the mode for any root by clicking on the root, alternating between hiding and showing its branches.

Release unused fonts when closing a document: Turning on this option, which is recommended, allows Interleaf 6 to free memory from unused parts of the font cache when a document is closed.

Evaluate attribute references continuously: If this option is on, attribute references are evaluated whenever you add, delete, or change the value of a token. This gives you immediate updates at the cost of slower performance. If this option is off, attribute references are evaluated only when you open, save, or print a document.

Adjust pair kerning when importing documents: If this option is on, pair kerning is done using the default settings when loading the following kinds of documents: Interleaf Release 3, ASCII documents with no markup (i.e., text files with a filename extension indicating a document class), and ASCII documents with markup but without font specifications.

Default when applying properties: This item offers you two choices, **Changes to Current** and **Changes to All**. Whichever is selected will be the default function for the **Apply** button on *Properties* dialog boxes for objects within a document.

Keep together at beginning of word: This specifies the number of characters that must be left in the first segment of a hyphenated word.

Keep together at end of word: This determines the number of characters that must be left in the last segment of a hyphenated word.

Check spelling when hyphenating: If this option is selected, words are only checked against the dictionary when they are entered, and are subsequently skipped during spell checking. If this button is off, each spelling check operation checks all words. This causes slower performance, but enables you to spell check text imported from ASCII files.

View Preferences

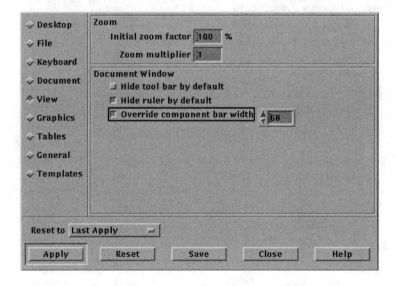

Initial zoom factor: This field specifies the zoom factor used when any document is opened.

Zoom multiplier: This must be a value from 0.25 to 16 that can be used to scale the display of document contents to conform to a particular display device, without affecting the zoom factors saved with documents. The product of a document's zoom factor and the value in this field is the effective zoom factor.

Hide tool bar by default: If this button is selected, the tool bar is hidden when any document is opened.

Hide ruler by default: If this button is selected, the rulers are hidden when any document is opened.

Override component bar width: If this button is selected, the up-down arrow field determines the width (in screen pixels) of the document component bar.

Graphics Preferences

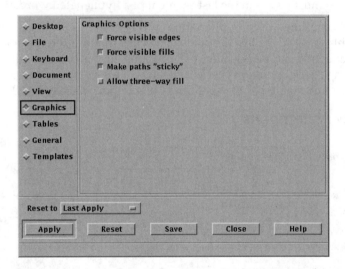

Force visible edges: If this button is on, then if a graphics object has its edge visible property turned off, and you change its edge color, weight, or pattern, the edge visible property of that object will be turned on.

Force visible fills: If you select this option, and a graphics object has its fill visible property turned off, and you change its fill weight or pattern, the fill visible property of that object will be turned on.

Make paths "sticky": If this button is on, stickiness locks will take effect: if two graphics objects are stickiness locked and one of them is moved, rotated, or resized, the other will be moved or resized so that they continue to touch. If this button is off, stickiness locks have no effect. Turning this button off does not clear stickiness locks; if you turn it back on, the locks will once again take effect.

Allow three-way fill: This option controls what Interleaf 6 does in certain situations when determining fills of graphics objects. It applies to situations in which regions are defined by three or more lines that intersect at a single point, creating an ambiguity in determining the fills of some regions. If this option is off, Interleaf will not fill the region of ambiguous fill. If this option is on, and you set a fill that would affect the ambiguous region, Interleaf 6 makes an arbitrary choice to resolve the ambiguity.

Tables Preferences

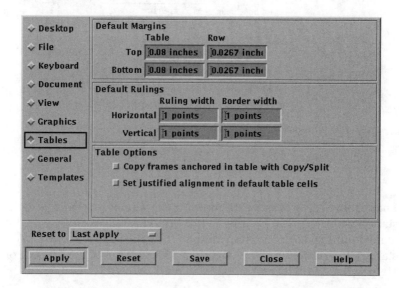

Default margins: This table of four fields defines the default top and bottom margins for tables and rows.

Default rulings: This table of four fields defines the default widths for horizontal and vertical table borders (the Border width column) and rulings between cells and between rows (the Ruling width column).

Copy frames anchored in table with Copy/Split: If this option is on, frames anchored in a table will be copied when the row(s) containing them are copied. Otherwise, such frames will be omitted from copied material.

↦ Note: Frames that are table cells are always copied. This option applies to frames that are anchored on a table row, but not within a cell. Frames may be anchored to the right of the right-most cell of a row.

Set justified alignment in default table cells: When this button is on, cells in tables created with the *(<New>)* menu entry (see page 47) are automatically made justified. Otherwise, they are left-justified.

General Preferences

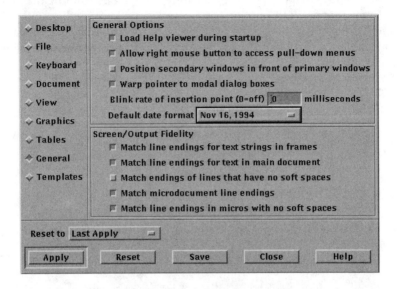

Load Help viewer during startup: If this option is on, WorldView is started when Interleaf 6 starts. If this button is off, WorldView is not loaded until you select a **Help** button. If WorldView is not loaded on startup, Interleaf 6 will start slightly more quickly, but the first use of **Help** will receive slower response.

Allow right mouse button to access pulldown menus: When this option is on, both the right and left mouse buttons can be used to pull down menus from menu bars.

Position secondary windows in front of primary windows: When this option is on, secondary document windows are always positioned in front of primary windows. For example, if a document is open and a *Create* dialog box for that document is also open, and the document's window overlaps the dialog box, the dialog box will always be on top of (obscure) the document window. If this option is *not* selected, either window may be above the other, under user control.

Warp pointer to modal dialog boxes: If you turn this option on, then when something you do causes Interleaf 6 to open a dialog box to which you must respond before doing anything else, the mouse pointer will automatically move into the dialog box.

Blink rate of insertion point:This field specifies the interval at which the text cursor blinks, in milliseconds. A value of zero will prevent blinking.

Default date format: This pulldown allows a choice of date formats for use when inserting a date in text via a key sequence. It also determines the format of the current date in some template documents, such as memos, supplied with Interleaf 6.

The next five buttons concern the accuracy of screen display of text. Due to differences in size between printer fonts (which control composition) and screen fonts, and to the presence of non–printing markers such as index tokens and frame anchors, lines of text displayed on the screen may not always seem to end at the correct place. None of these settings affects the printed appearance of the text.

Match line endings for text strings in frames: When this option is on, line endings of text strings in frames will be accurately displayed on the screen.

Match line endings for text in main document: When this feature is selected, line endings of text in the main body of the document (outside of frames) will be accurately displayed on the screen.

Match endings of lines that have no soft spaces: If you select this option, line endings of text containing only a single word (i.e., no soft spaces) will be accurately displayed on the screen.

Match microdocument line endings: If you select this option, line endings of text in components within frames will be accurately displayed on the screen.

Match line endings in micros with no soft spaces: If you select this option, line endings of text in components that contain no soft spaces within frames will be accurately displayed on the screen.

Templates Preferences

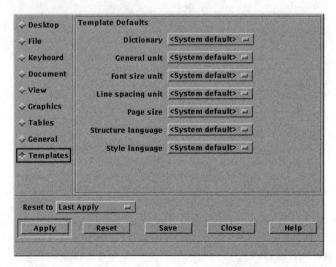

Dictionary: This pulldown offers a list of all available dictionaries, including No Dictionary.

General unit: This pulldown offers a list of all available units of measure for general use.

Font size unit: This pulldown offers a list of all available units of measure for display of font information.

Line spacing: This pulldown offers a list of all available units of measure for display of line spacing (interline leading).

Page size: This pulldown offers a list of all available page size codes, for example, letter and A4.

Structure language: This pulldown offers a list of all available languages in which components, frames, and streams can be named when you create a new document.

Style language: This pulldown offers a list of all available languages that can determine the page margins of a newly created document.

Print

ACCESS: Desktop menu bar: File→Print
             Document menu bar: File→Print
             Text tool bar

FUNCTION: Print documents, host files, or containers

⚭ Note: Interleaf 6 for Windows follows Windows conventions for the user interface to printing.

A *Print* dialog box is opened:

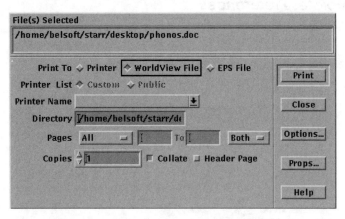

Some fields of this dialog box are useful only for Interleaf 6 documents and are inaccessible if any of the icons to be printed are not Interleaf 6 documents or containers.

The read-only Files(s) Selected subwindow displays the paths of all icons selected for printing.

The **Print To** radio buttons specify the available types of output. **Printer** causes output to be directed to the printer specified in the **Printer Name** pulldown. **WorldView File** causes creation of a file (in Printerleaf format) that can be displayed by WorldView. This file will appear as an icon in the container specified in the **Directory** field. **EPS File** specifies creation of an Encapsulated PostScript file, which will also appear as an icon in the container specified in the **Directory** field.

The **Printer Name** pulldown displays the printer to be used if the **Printer** radio button is selected. Clicking the select button on this pulldown displays a selectable list of printers. The contents of this list are determined by the two **Printer List** radio buttons, **Custom** and **Public** (see page 102).

The **Directory** field displays the path to which WorldView and EPS files are to be written. It is initialized to the container in which icons were selected for printing, but can be modified.

The Pages pulldown gives you three choices for the pages to be printed. *All* prints all pages of the document file. *Current* prints only the current page (which is the page that was current when the document was closed if you open this dialog box with a closed document icon selected). *Range* activates the numeric page number fields on either side of the label **To**. The left and right fields specify the low and high page number of the range to print. When you are printing more than one page, the pulldown to the right of these fields allows you to select *Even* (print even-numbered pages only), *Odd* (print odd-numbered pages only), or *Both* (print all pages).

The **Copies** field specifies how many copies to print. The **Collate** button determines whether or not to collate when the **Copies** field is set to more than one.

The **Print** button on the right side of the dialog box initiates printing.

The **Options...** button on the right side of the dialog box opens a printer control dialog box (see page 100).

The **Props...** button on the right side of the dialog box opens a print properties dialog box:

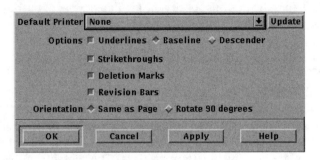

These properties apply to the current document and are saved with it if it is saved.

Default Printer: This pulldown lists all defined printers. The printer initially displayed on this pulldown is the default and is displayed in the **Printer Name** field of the *Print* dialog box when first opened. The default applies only to the current document. The **Update** button resets the pulldown to the initial value.

Options: These buttons control whether or not the listed attributes will be applied when text is printed. If **Underline** is selected, the **Baseline** and **Descender** radio buttons give a choice of position. These options do not affect whether or not text is printed, but only whether or not the specified attribute is used. If **Spot Color Separations** is selected, the **Screened** and **Solid** radio buttons give a choice of two methods.

Orientation Same as Page: If this button is on, the document is printed in the orientation determined by the *Document Properties* dialog box (see page 51).

Rotate 90 degrees: If you select this option, the document is printed in an orientation rotated 90 degrees from that specified by the *Document Properties* dialog box (see page 51).

Printer options

ACCESS: Print dialog box Options button

FUNCTION: Set printer-specific parameters

➤ **Note:** Interleaf 6 for Windows follows Windows conventions for the user interface to printer options.

A *Printer Options* dialog box opens. This dialog box has two pages, **Basic** and **Advanced**.

This is the **Basic** printer control page:

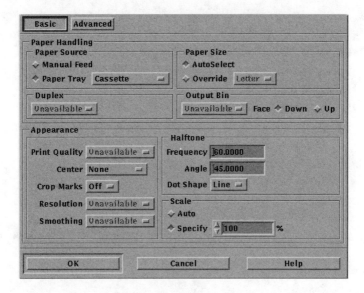

This is the **Advanced** printer control page:

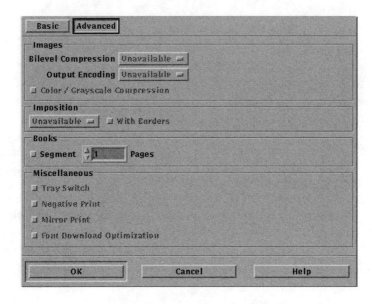

The effect of each of these controls is specific to the printer in use (see page 102).

Print setup

ACCESS: Desktop menu bar: File→Print Setup
Document menu bar: File→Print Setup

FUNCTION: Add, change, or remove system printers, or specify default printer

•● **Note:** Interleaf 6 for Windows follows Windows conventions for the user interface to print setup.

A *Print Setup* dialog box is opened:

This dialog box, with four pages, adds and removes printer definitions, changes print parameters, and sets the default printer. The **Change** page, pictured above, has all the fields of this dialog box. The other pages have the same layout, but some fields are not on all pages. On the **Add** page, the line containing the **Custom** and **Public** buttons is labeled **Add to Menu** rather than **Add**.

The list of names in the Printer Menu Name pulldown defines the list of printers that will appear in the **Printer Name** field of a *Print* dialog box (see page 98).

Custom and **Public**: These radio buttons determine whether the list of printers displayed in the **Printer Menu Name** field is the public list or your custom list.

Add: If this option is selected, the **Add to Menu** label is visible (otherwise, this label is **Menu**). The name of a printer can be entered in the **Printer Menu Name** field for creation of a new printer menu entry.

Change: A printer can be selected from the Printer Menu Name pulldown to change fields pertaining to that printer. A new name can be entered in the Printer Menu Name pulldown to change the printer name.

Copy to Custom Menu: This button copies a printer definition from the public list to your custom list. This allows you to create your own variation of that definition without changing the public printer.

Remove: If this button is selected, a printer can be selected from the Printer Menu Name pulldown and removed from the system.

Default: If this button is selected, a printer can be selected from the **Printer Menu Name** pulldown and will become the default printer displayed in the **Printer Name** field of a *Print* dialog box.

Print To Printer or **File**: These radio buttons determine whether output goes by default to a physical printer or a disk file.

Filter Print Job On Desktop, Client or **Server**: If **Print to Printer** is selected, these radio buttons determine where processing to prepare the document for the specified printer is performed.

Printer Location Local or **Remote**: These radio buttons specify whether the printer is a local or a remote printer.

Remote Print Server: This field may be entered only if **Printer Location Remote** is selected.

Printer Queue Name: This field must be the one-word operating system queue name for the printer.

Printer Type PostScript or **PCL**: These radio buttons determine whether the printer named in the **Printer Menu Name** field is a PostScript printer or a PCL printer. This determines the names displayed on the Printer Model pulldown below these buttons.

Printer Model: This pulldown displays the available printer models corresponding to the selected printer type, PostScript or PCL.

Set Printer Options: This button opens a *Set Printer Options* dialog box:

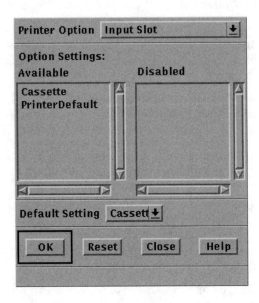

Printer Option: The pulldown menu of this field displays a list of all printer options. The remaining fields on this dialog box affect the setting of the option displayed in this field.

Available and **Disabled**: These lists define which settings of the current option are permitted for the current printer and which are disabled. Selecting an item in one list moves it to the other. Disabled settings are not listed on the *Options* dialog box of the *Print* dialog box.

Default setting: The pulldown menu of this field displays a list of all settings defined for the selected option. The setting displayed in this field is the default and is displayed on the *Options* dialog box of the *Print* dialog box when first opened.

Publish document

ACCESS: Document File pulldown: Publish

FUNCTION: Access dialog boxes for graphics settings

This menu selection allows you to distribute copies of the current document in several formats. An *Interleaf Publish* dialog box opens:

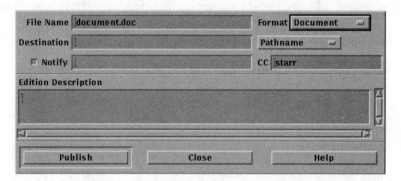

The **File Name** field specifies the name to give the published copy. It is initialized to the name of the current document, but you can modify it to publish the document with a different name. The Format pulldown allows you to select the format of the copy that will be published. *Document* publishes an Interleaf 6 document, including its part files. *PostScript* converts the document to PostScript. *WorldView* converts the document to WorldView format (equivalent to an Interleaf 5 Printerleaf file). *Read-Only* converts the document to WorldView format that can be viewed onscreen but not printed.

The **Destination** line specifies where the published copy of the document should go. If you select *Pathname* on the pulldown, you must supply the path of a directory (without a filename) in the text field. Otherwise, select *Desktop* to place the output on users' desktops, or *Bulletin Board* to place it in bulletin boards, and enter the destination users' names, separated by spaces, in the text fields.

If **Notify** is on, notifications will be sent by electronic mail when publication is complete, to the e-mail addresses listed in the field to the right. A copy of the notification will be sent to the user named in the **CC** field. **Edition Description** is free-form text that will be included in the notification.

Click the **Publish** button to complete the operation. The next time you publish the document, the **File Name**, **Format**, **Destination**, and **Notify** settings you used will be retained as the initial values of these fields.

Read Eval Lisp commands

ACCESS: Desktop menu bar: Tools→Read-Eval
            Text tool bar

FUNCTION: Evaluate Lisp expressions

A window is opened in which the user may type Lisp expressions. These are evaluated and the results are displayed in the window.

Revert to document

ACCESS: Document menu bar: File→Revert to

FUNCTION: Open saved version or older version of document

The current open document's contents are replaced by the permanent saved version, backup version, or checkpoint version, whichever is available and selected by the operator. Any changes that have been made since the last save are lost. The operator is prompted for confirmation before any changes are discarded.

➥ **Note:** The version to which you have reverted is not automatically saved. For example, if you open a document, revert to backup, and close, the backup does not become the current version. If you revert to backup and then save, the backup does become current.

Revision Tracking

ACCESS: Document menu bar Tools pulldown

FUNCTION: Control Revision Tracking

A *Revision Tracking* dialog box is opened:

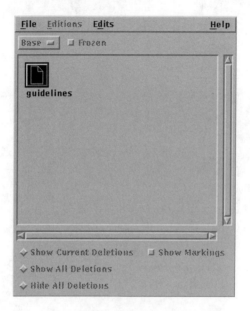

Select *Add Edit* on the Edits pulldown to open an *Add Edit* dialog box:

By entering an edit name and selecting **Add**, you create a new edit. The new edit is made the *active* edit.

When you first create an edit, Revision Tracking is enabled. Additions and changes to the document are tracked and are associated with the current edit, until you create a new edit. By using *Add Edit* on the Edits pulldown again, you can create another edit, which becomes active. Edits are displayed vertically in sequence as icons on the *Revision Tracking* dialog box:

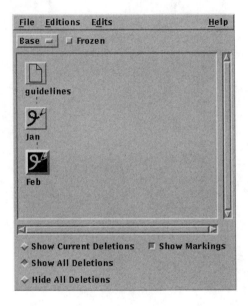

By selecting the icon for an edit *not* at the bottom of the sequence, and then executing *Add Edit* on the Edits pulldown, you can create a branch in the sequence of edits, beneath the selected edit. For example, by selecting the **Jan** edit, and adding an edit named **Jan-01**, you could create the following edit structure:

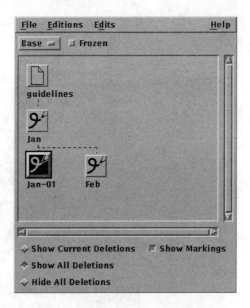

Jan-01 and **Feb** are now *parallel edits*. Material that is created when one of them is active cannot be deleted or modified when the other is active, unless you suspend Revision Tracking.

When an edit's icon is selected in the *Revision Tracking* dialog box, you can access the Edits pulldown. This has six entries:

Add Edit	As described above, this opens an *Add Edit* dialog box.
Properties	This opens an *Edit Properties* dialog box:

This dialog box has two pages, controlled by the Text Highlighting When pulldown. With this pulldown, you select the **Active Edit** page, for properties to be used when this edit is the active edit, or the **Inactive Edit** page, for properties to be used when this edit is not active. Each of these pages has an **Insertion Markup** section, in which you set the text properties and color used to denote added text, and a **Deletion Markup** section, for setting text properties and color to denote removed text. Thus, you can distinguish between added and removed text, and also between different edits.

If the **Frozen** button on this dialog box is on, text entered in this edit cannot be removed or changed, unless you suspend Revision Tracking.

Attributes

This opens an *Attributes* dialog box (see page 18):

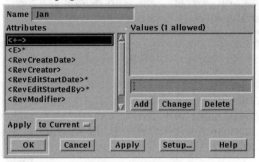

The attributes whose names begin and end with angle brackets (<>) are used by the Revision Tracking system and cannot be modified. However, you can select the **Setup** button and create your own attributes (see page 20). You can modify the values of these.

Exclude/Include

These menu entries toggle. Selecting *Exclude* causes all changes belonging to this edit to disappear from the display, although the content of the document does not change, and the *Include* choice appears. Selecting *Include* reverses the process. These menu choices also allow you to move edits between editions, as described below

Activate

This makes the selected edit become active. If you select *Exclude*, this edit cannot be made active until you select *Include*.

Delete

This menu choice allows you to delete the selected edit or all edits not currently in use (those excluded using the *Exclude* menu item). The *Delete* menu choice is not available unless the selected edit has been excluded using *Exclude*.

A document in which Revision Tracking has been enabled may have many editions, each of which may contain many edits. Existing editions in the current document are listed in a pulldown on the *Revision Tracking* dialog box. In the illustration of this dialog box on page 107, this pulldown is in the upper left and is labeled **Base**, the initial edition. You can create new editions using the *Create New Edition* choice on the

Editions pulldown, or by entering a new edition name on the *Add Edit* dialog box (see page 107). Using the pulldown, you can make any existing edition current. New edits belong to whichever edition is current when the edits are created.

Next to the pulldown is the edition **Frozen** toggle button, which freezes or unfreezes the current edition, and optionally, all of its edits.

Edits belonging to an edition that is lower on the pulldown than the current edition (i.e., edits that belong to a newer edition) are displayed as grayed icons and cannot be made active. However, you can select such an icon, and then select Edits→Include to place the edit in the current edition.

A *baseline* is a separate document file version of a document. You create a new baseline by selecting *Create Baseline* on the Editions pulldown of the *Revision Tracking* dialog box. A *Create Baseline* dialog box is opened:

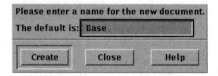

Enter a new name, if desired, and press **Create**. A new copy is made of the current document, with the specified name, and is opened; the previously open document is closed. In the new document, Revision Tracking is initially suspended, and all material belongs to one edition and edit. In other words, the new baseline contains the same effective content as the previous document, with all Revision Tracking information removed.

File→Suspend on the *Revision Tracking* dialog box suspends Revision Tracking, allowing you to make changes regardless of which material belongs to any edit or whether edits or editions are frozen. File→Resume resumes Revision Tracking. File→Close closes the dialog box.

Rulers visibility

ACCESS: Document menu bar: View→Rulers

FUNCTION: Show or hide rulers in document window

If the rulers are currently visible in the current document, they are hidden; if hidden, they are made visible.

Save document

ACCESS: 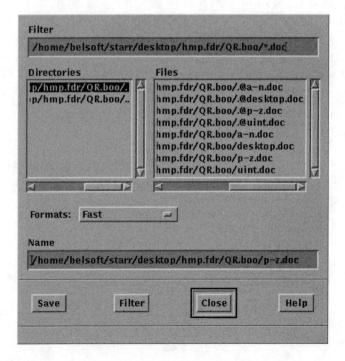 Document menu bar: File→Save
Text tool bar

FUNCTION: Save document to file

Note: Interleaf 6 for Windows follows Windows conventions for the user interface to saving files.

The current document is saved (written to disk storage as a permanent version). The previously saved version, if any, becomes the backup version, and the previous backup version, if any, is deleted.

Save as document

ACCESS: Document menu bar: File→Save As. . .

FUNCTION: Save document to file with choice of formats

Note: Interleaf 6 for Windows follows Windows conventions for the user interface to saving files.

The current document is saved (written to disk storage as a permanent version) with a choice of storage formats.

A *Save As* dialog box is opened:

This dialog box, which operates as a *File Selection* dialog box (see page 116), has a **Save** button. It also has a Formats pulldown, which lists available save formats (see page 89 and following, the File subsection, for information on changing this list).

Select in document

ACCESS: Document menu bar: Edit→Select
            Component bar menu

FUNCTION: Select document content for further operations

This menu choice allows selecting top-level components (including table rows). It brings up a submenu of nine choices: *All, All of...*, *Toggle*, *through Page...*, *to Beginning, to End, Previous, Next*, and *Pasted Text* (*Toggle, Previous, Next*, and *Pasted Text* are not available from the component bar). The effect of each choice depends on context: if a frame or table cell is currently open, all operations are within the current micro-document only. Otherwise, all operations apply to top-level components within the current document. In either case, the top-level components in question are those shown in the component bar.

With the exception of *Toggle, Previous*, and *Next*, these operations do not deselect any components. This makes it possible to build up a selection using several methods or using one method repeatedly. For example, with *All of...*, it is possible to obtain a selection of multiple component names at one time.

All: This selects all top-level components (including all table rows) in the document, whether or not any were initially selected.

All of: This brings up a *Select* dialog box listing either non-row components or table rows, depending on whether or not the component bar cursor is within a table:

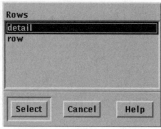

Pressing the **Select** button causes all components with the highlighted name to be selected.

Toggle: All currently selected components are deselected, and all other top-level components are selected.

Through Page: A dialog box is opened for entry of a page number:

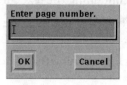

If the page number entered specifies a page following the current page, all components from the component bar cursor position to the end of the specified page are selected. If the page number entered specifies a page before the current page, all components from the component bar cursor position to the beginning of the specified page are selected. If the number entered specifies the current page, all components from the component bar cursor position to the end of the current page are selected.

To Beginning: All components from the component bar cursor position to the beginning of the document are selected.

To End: All components from the component bar cursor position to the end of the document are selected.

Previous: Any selected components are deselected, and the component preceding the current component bar cursor position is selected.

Next: Any selected components are deselected, and the component following the current component bar cursor position is selected.

Pasted Text: This choice is available immediately after a paste has been done in the text area (not in the component bar). It causes the pasted text to be selected.

Select all icons

ACCESS: Desktop menu bar: Edit→Select All

FUNCTION: Select a container's contents

All icons in the current container are selected.

Select cells in table

ACCESS: Document menu bar: Tables→Select Cells

FUNCTION: Select table cells for further operations

This menu choice allows selecting cells within a single table. It brings up a submenu of five choices: *Current Cell, in Current Column, in Current Row, All Cells*, and *Toggle*.

Any movement of the text cursor from one cell to another deselects any selected cells. Therefore, it is *not* possible to build up a selection of cells by repeated use of this menu item.

Current Cell: The cell containing the text cursor is selected.

In Current Column: The cell containing the text cursor, and all cells in the same column, are selected.

In Current Row: The cell containing the text cursor, and all cells in the same row, are selected.

All Cells: This selects all cells in all rows in the table.

Toggle: All currently selected cells in the current table are deselected, and all its other cells are selected.

Select file for operation

ACCESS: Various file operation menus

FUNCTION: Select file (desktop icon)

This dialog box is opened by a variety of commands which open files or select files for processing. This section is referenced in the descriptions of those commands.

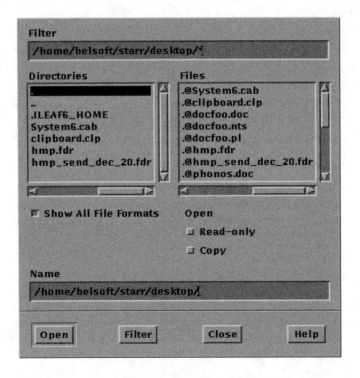

This dialog box is used to select a file by name rather than by icon. The text field labeled **Filter** contains a path specification, possibly including wildcard characters. This field is initialized to specify some or all of the files in the container from which the File pulldown was selected, and may be modified by the user.

In the **Filter** field, the asterisk is a wildcard character and can stand for any combination of other characters. For example, "c*.doc" specifies any document (file with a ".doc" extension) whose name begins with the letter "c."

The scrollable subwindow labeled **Directories** lists all directories whose paths fit the specification in the **Filter** field.

The scrollable subwindow labeled Files lists all directories whose paths fit the specification in the **Filter** field.

⇥ **Note:** Files within the directories listed in the Directories subwindow are not listed.

To change the path specification in the **Filter** field, either (1) select the field and edit its contents, or (2) select a path from the Directories subwindow, which copies the selected path to the **Filter** field.

To update the selections in the Directories and Files subwindows after changing the **Filter** field, press the **Filter** button at the bottom of the dialog box.

◆ **Tip:** By successively selecting paths in the Directories subwindow and pressing the **Filter** button, you can search in a directory structure for a desired file.

Select rows in table

ACCESS: Component bar menu
             Document menu bar: Tables→Select Rows

FUNCTION: Select table rows for further operations

This menu choice allows selecting rows within a single table. It brings up a submenu of six choices: *All Rows in Table, Rows through Page..., To Beginning of Table, To End of Table, All of...*, and *Toggle*. The Document menu bar Tables pulldown offers an additional choice, *Current Row*, which selects the row containing the text cursor.

Aside from *Toggle*, these operations do not deselect any rows. This makes it possible to build up a selection using several methods or using one method repeatedly. For example, with repeated *All of...* selections, it is possible to obtain a selection of multiple row names at one time.

➥ **Note:** This menu item is available *only* if the component bar cursor is within a table *and* there are no currently selected top-level components (including table rows) outside of this table.

All: This selects all rows in the table, whether or not any were initially selected.

All of...: This brings up a *Select* dialog box listing only names of rows within the current table:

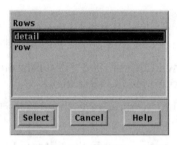

Pressing the **Select** button causes all rows with the highlighted name to be selected.

Toggle: All currently selected rows in the current table are deselected, and all its other rows are selected.

Rows through Page: A dialog box is opened for entry of a page number:

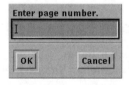

If the page number entered specifies a page following the current page, all rows from the component bar cursor position to the end of the specified page or the end of the table are selected. If the page number entered specifies a page before the current page, all rows from the component bar cursor position to the beginning of the specified page or the beginning of the table are selected. If the number entered specifies the current page, all rows from the component bar cursor position to the end of the current page or of the table are selected.

To Beginning of Table: All rows from the component bar cursor position to the beginning of the table are selected.

To End of Table: All rows from the component bar cursor position to the end of the table are selected.

Select Toggle icons

ACCESS: Desktop menu bar: Edit→Select Toggle

FUNCTION: Toggle selection of a container's contents

All currently selected icons in the current container are deselected, and all unselected icons are selected.

Shape Text

ACCESS: Document menu bar: Tools→Shape Text

FUNCTION: Set indents of text lines

A *Shape Text* dialog box opens:

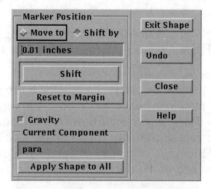

The beginning and ending positions of text lines on the screen are marked with vertical gray bars. Using the mouse, you can select or more of these markers. Selected markers become black vertical bars. Then, you can adjust the positions of the selected markers. The indents of the lines are adjusted so that the lines now begin and end at the new marker positions. Since you can adjust both ends of each line independently, you can cause the block of text to take any desired shape.

There are three ways you can do this:

First, you can drag the selected markers with the mouse.

Second, you can press the **Shift by** radio button and enter a value in the numeric field beneath the button. When you select the **Shift** button, all selected markers will move by the specified distance. Enter a negative distance to move to the left.

Last, you can press the **Move to** radio button and enter a value in the numeric field. The **Shift** button in the illustration will become a **Move** button. Pressing it will cause selected markers to move to the specified position. Distances are measured relative to the zero point on the horizontal ruler. Negative values are move to the left. If you have selected markers that are in different horizontal positions, one of them will move to the specified position, and the others will keep their positions in relation to that one. If you select beginning and end of line markers simultaneously and execute **Move to**, the command will be executed within the limits of the page margins, but the result may not be useful.

The **Reset to Margins** button moves all selected marks to their default positions.

If **Gravity** is on, any mark that is dragged and released close to another mark on the line immediately above and below will snap to a position aligned with that mark. Otherwise, any mark will remain where it is released. This option does not affect the positioning of marks with **Shift** and **Move**.

If you select **Apply Shape to All**, the current shaping information will be applied to all components with the name in the **Current Component** field.

↦ **Note:** You can close the *Shape Text* dialog box by pressing **Close**, but you will remain in Shape Text mode. You can still drag markers to change shape, but you will be unable to do ordinary text editing in the current document. To exit Shape Text mode, you must press **Exit Shape**. You can reopen the dialog box with Tools→Shape Text on the document menu bar.

Size container

ACCESS: Desktop menu bar: View→Full Size

FUNCTION: Change size of a container's window

Selecting the **Full Size** button causes the current container's window to be sized according to its contents, after which the **Full Size** button is replaced by the **Restore Size** button. Selecting the **Restore Size** button causes the current container's window to revert to its most recent user-defined size, after which the **Restore Size** button is replaced by the **Full Size** button.

Spelling check

ACCESS: 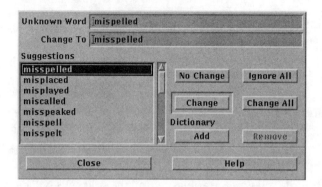 Document menu bar: Tools→Spelling
Text tool bar

FUNCTION: Check spelling of document text

A *Spelling* dialog box is opened:

Unknown Word	mispelled
Change To	misspelled

Suggestions

misspelled		No Change	Ignore All
misplaced			
misplayed			
miscalled		Change	Change All
misspeaked			
misspell		Dictionary	
misspelt		Add	Remove

Close	Help

Words in the document that do not match the applicable dictionary are displayed one after the other in the **Unknown Word** field. Suggested corrections from the dictionary are listed under **Suggestions**. By selecting the **Change** button, you cause the highlighted suggestion to replace the misspelled word. You can also click on the **Change to** field and modify the suggested replacement before selecting **Change**. **Change All** changes all occurrences of the unknown word in the current document.

In the **Dictionary** group, **Add** adds the unknown word to your desktop dictionary, so that it is considered to be a correct spelling. If a word that you have added appears in the **Suggestions** list, you can click on that word and activate the **Remove** button. Selecting **Remove** then removes the word from your desktop dictionary. You cannot remove words from the system dictionary.

No Change causes spell checking to continue, skipping this occurrence of the unknown word. **Ignore All** causes all occurrences of the unknown word to be skipped in this document, without modifying your dictionary.

➥ **Note:** If there is a text selection at the time you select the spelling check tool, only the selected text will be checked. If the selected text contains no errors, the spelling dialog box will not open. If there are errors, the dialog box will open. When all errors in the selection have been processed, you will be asked whether or not you want to continue with the rest of the document.

- **Note:** If a microdocument is open, you will be offered the choice of checking only within that microdocument or of continuing with the entire document.

◆ **Tip:** To prevent a section of text from being spell checked, select it, and set its **Dictionary** property to *<No Dictionary>* using the *Text Properties* dialog box (see page 129).

Split cell in table

ACCESS: Document menu bar: Tables→Split Cell

FUNCTION: Split a straddle cell in a table

The text cursor must be within a straddle cell (see page 80). The cell borders that disappeared when this straddle was created appear as flashing dashed lines, and the text cursor becomes a table ruling cursor. By clicking the left mouse button over a flashing border segment, you cause the straddle cell to be split at that point.

If the straddle cell was a graphics cell, all the split cells will be graphics cells. This will be the case by default if any of the original cells was a graphic cell. The straddle cell may also have been made a graphics cell after the straddle was created.

- **Note:** If the straddle contains only two original cells, no flashing borders appear. The cell is simply split.

◆ **Tip:** The contents of the cell that is split are replicated in full in both the cells into which it is split. It is possible that some of the straddle cell's content may be shifted out of view in the split cells. It is still there and can be recovered by shifting (if a graphics cell) or setting the cell's **Size to Width** property.

- **Note:** If a straddle cell has graphic content (other than text strings or microdocuments), and you set its **Editor** property to **Object** before you split it, the graphic content will *not* be replicated in the split.

Split table

ACCESS: Document menu bar: Tables→Split Table

FUNCTION: Split a table between rows

The component bar cursor must be in a table.

The current table is split at the point indicated by the component bar cursor. If you split a table containing header or footer rows, these will be replicated in the new tables.

◆ **Tip:** To avoid confusion in determining where the split will take place, it is recommended that you not have any rows selected when doing a split. Instead, place the component bar cursor between the rows at the point you wish the split to take place.

Sync book

ACCESS: Desktop menu bar: Book pulldown

FUNCTION: Update book summary information

Books maintain some information that span the documents (and possibly sub-books) within them. This information is necessary for Table of Contents (TOC) and index generation and includes page numbers, effectivity, and references. A TOC or an index is of no value unless it accurately reflects the entries and page numbers within the book. Opening and modifying any one document within the book may have an impact on information in or the composition of other documents within the book. Cutting a document from the book or pasting a new document into the book will have the same effect. A *sync* (synchronize) operation ensures that all this information is current.

A prompt is opened:

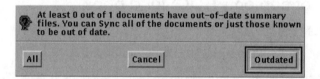

If documents or sub-books are selected within the current book, the *sync* operation applies only to them, or else all documents and sub-books within the current book are affected. The operation will not proceed if any open documents are selected. You can *sync* the entire book or just the part that Interleaf 6 is certain is out of date.

When the operation is finished, Interleaf 6 displays a message telling you how many documents were opened.

Tab fill

ACCESS: Document menu bar: Edit→Tab Fill

FUNCTION: Change fill of tabs in document text

This menu selection is for changing the fill of tabs, that is, the appearance of the space that is occupied by a tab. It brings up a tear-off menu:

This menu lists the five available patterns. "Blank" stands for blank fill (no pattern). If there is a text selection, and one of the listed patterns is selected, all tabs in the selection are given the selected fill. Whether or not there is a text selection, all tabs created in the document from then on will have the selected fill, until another fill is selected.

Table of contents (TOC) for a book

SELECTION: Yes

ACCESS: Desktop menu bar: Book pulldown

FUNCTION: Generate a Table of Contents for a book

This menu selection generates a Table of Contents for the current book.

◆ **Tip:** It is recommended that you execute a Book→Sync before generating a TOC, to ensure that all information is up to date.

Table properties

ACCESS: Document menu bar: Properties→Table
            Component bar: Properties menu

FUNCTION: Change properties of a table

A *Table Properties* dialog box opens:

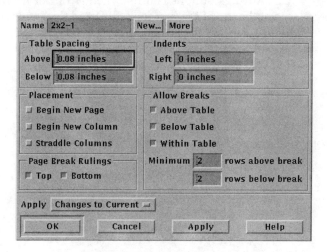

The **Table Spacing** fields define margins of empty space that must be left above and below the table, reducing the number of rows that may fit in a column. The **Indents** fields specify empty space that must be left at the sides of the table, reducing the possible width of the table.

➥ **Note:** The **Above** and **Below** spacing fields apply only at the top (beginning) and bottom (end) of the entire table, not to each page or column on which a section of the table is placed.

In the **Placement** section, the **Begin New Page** toggle button forces the table to the top of a page, starting a new page if necessary. The **Begin New Column** button forces the table to the top of a column, beginning a new column (and possibly a new page) if necessary. The **Straddle Columns** button allows the table to stretch all the way across a multi-column page.

In the **Allow Breaks** section, buttons and fields define composition parameters that Interleaf 6 will try to observe, though it may not be possible to do so in some cases. **Above Table**, if off, specifies that the table should be on the same page as the preceding component. **Below Table**, if off, specifies that the next component should be on the same page as the end of this table. **Within Table**, if off, specifies that all of this table should be in the same page and column (which may force a column or page break). The **Minimum of rows below/above break** fields specify the minimum number of rows at the beginning or end of this table that should be isolated from the rest of the table by a column (or page) break; in other words, the smallest fraction of the table that should be alone on a page or column.

The **Page Break Rulings** buttons control whether or not horizontal rules are placed at the top of the first row (**Top**) and the bottom of the last row (**Bottom**) adjacent to page or column breaks within the table. These controls apply *only* at breaks within the table, not to the first and last rows of the table.

Table cell properties

ACCESS: Document menu bar: Properties pulldown

FUNCTION: Change properties of a table cell

A *Cell Properties* dialog box opens:

There are two options for **Height** (vertical extent of the cell). **Contents** sets the height according to the cell contents (even if a cell is empty, the properties defined for any text that might be entered will determine a vertical extent, as with an empty top-level component). **Fixed** allows you to enter a fixed numeric value. When you switch from **Contents** to **Fixed**, the **Fixed** field initially contains the value determined by the contents.

➬ **Note:** Reducing the Fixed height of a cell, or reducing its height by changing its contents or content properties, will not necessarily change its apparent height. All cells on a row will have the same height when the row is composed, and the vertical extent of the row will be determined by the tallest cell on the row.

Editor also offers two options. If **Graphics** is selected, when you double-click on the cell, it will be opened as a graphics frame, with a gray border. If **Object** is selected, the component content of the cell immediately appears in the component bar, and you can work with the properties and contents of the components.

If **Editor** is **Graphics**, the cell may contain microdocuments. If so, and **Size to Width** is on, the horizontal extents of microdocuments will be adjusted if you change the cell's width. This allows text to be efficiently composed within the cell. Otherwise, space may be wasted if the cell is wider than the microdocument, or text may be obscured if the microdocument is wider.

If **Editor** is **Graphics** and **Size to Height** is on, and **Height** is **Fixed**, graphical content of the cell (excluding text strings and microdocuments) will be resized vertically to fit the vertical extent of the cell whenever the cell is closed.

The **Background** section allows you to specify a background color and pattern that will fill the cell behind its contents. The default is solid white. The **Color** and **Pattern** buttons open the appropriate palettes. The **Visible** toggle button enables you to change between your specified color and pattern and the default of solid white, without having to clear your specification.

◆ **Tip:** Every table cell contains at least one component, and possibly more. In general, these components contain the text content of the cell. By opening the cell and then selecting *Component...* on the document menu bar Properties pulldown, you can modify the properties of these components.

There are three radio buttons in the **Vertical Alignment** section, **Top**, **Center**, and **Bottom**. Selecting one of these can cause the cell contents to be positioned to the top of the cell, vertically centered within the cell, or placed at the bottom of the cell. However, these properties do not take effect (and alignment to the top is used) unless the cell is larger in vertical extent than its contents. This happens if another cell in the same row has a greater height than this one requires, forcing this one to a larger height.

Table row properties

ACCESS: Document menu bar: Properties→Row
            Component bar: Properties menu

FUNCTION: Change properties of a table row

A *Row Properties* dialog box opens:

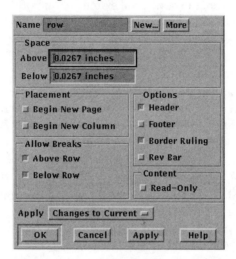

The **Space** fields define margins of empty space that must be left above and below the contents of the row. This is equivalent to specifying top and bottom margins for the contents of each cell in the row. Increasing these values increases the vertical extent of each row, reducing the number of rows that may fit in a column.

In the **Placement** section, the **Begin New Page** toggle button forces the row to the top of a page, starting a new page if necessary. The **Begin New Column** button forces the row to the top of a column, beginning a new column (and possibly a new page) if necessary.

In the **Allow Breaks** section, buttons and fields define composition parameters that Interleaf 6 will try to observe, though this may not be possible in all cases. **Above Row**, if off, specifies that the row should be on the same page as the preceding row. **Below Row**, if off, specifies that the next row should be on the same page as this row.

Table rows may be designated as header and footer rows using the **Header** and **Footer** buttons in the **Options** area. Header rows appear at the tops of sections of the table, that is, immediately after page or column breaks. Footer rows appear at the bottoms of sections of the table, immediately before page or column breaks. A header row only takes effect at breaks *below* the initial occurrence of the row, so if you want a header to appear over all parts of a table, the header row must appear above all non-header rows. Similarly, a footer row takes effect only at breaks *above* its initial appearance. Only the initial occurrence of a header or footer row the instance whose properties you open to select **Header** or **Footer** may be selected or edited. The repeat occurrences generated at breaks are visible and will print but are read-only.

At any point in the table, you can create a new instance of a row whose name matches that of a header row, make the new row a header, and change its contents. The new row replaces the previous header of the same name at the next break. This allows you to partition a table into logical sections with varying headings. Since a table may have several different header rows with different names, you can create a system of nested headings at different levels.

◆ **Tip:** It is not required that header and footer rows have unique names, but it is recommended to avoid confusion. This is particularly true if a varying heading scheme such as the one described above is in use.

The **Rev Bar** button determines whether or not the row should have a revision bar. **Border Ruling** specifies whether or not the vertical borders at the left and right sides of the row should be visible.

In the **Content** section, you can set the **Read-Only** radio button to prevent the row from being modified by the operator.

Text properties

ACCESS: Document menu bar: Properties→Text
            Graphics tool palette: Text dialog box

FUNCTION: Change properties of text in a document

A *Text Properties* dialog box opens:

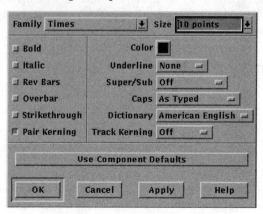

The **Family** pulldown lists the available font families, and allows you to select a new default font for the current component. The Size pulldown lists available sizes up to 36 point, and lets you type in sizes from 2 to 200. The **Color** button brings up a *Color* dialog box (see page 178). Toggle buttons control text properties **Bold**, **Italic**, **Rev Bars**, **Overbar**, **Strikethrough**, and **Pair Kerning**. The Underline pulldown offers a choice of *None*, *Single*, and *Double*. The Super/Sub pulldown offers a choice of *Superscript*, *Subscript*, or *Off* (neither).

Capitalization (**Caps**) can be *As Typed*, *Small Caps* (first letter), *All Small Caps*, or *All Caps*. The *As Typed* choice reverts to the operator-entered capitalization.

◆ **Tip:** Interleaf 6 "remembers" what you typed even after you save and close the document. You can always recover the capitalization as you typed it by selecting *As Typed*.

The Dictionary pulldown lists available dictionaries and *<No Dictionary>*. **Track Kerning** may be *Off* or have any of three values of looseness or three values of tightness.

The **Use Component Defaults** button sets the properties of the current text selection to match those of the component containing the text. Enclosing components may be referenced for inherited properties of nested inlines.

Tool Bar visibility

ACCESS: Document menu bar: View→Tool Bar

FUNCTION: Hide or show document tool bars

If the tool bar is currently visible in the header of the current document, it is hidden; if hidden, it is made visible. Both the text and graphics tool bars are affected, even though only one can be displayed at a time.

Tool Manager

SELECTION: No

ACCESS: Desktop menu bar: Tools→Admin→Tool Manager

FUNCTION: Start the Tool Manager to install or remove layered applications

The Tool Manager window is opened, allowing the user to install or remove layered applications. Available layered applications are determined by the contents of the Interleaf 6 Apps directory. Some layered applications supplied by Interleaf are options, and layered applications are available from sources other than Interleaf.

Transpose icons

SELECTION: Yes

ACCESS: Desktop menu bar: View→Transpose Icons

FUNCTION: Reposition desktop icons

The selected icons are repositioned so that each one takes the position of the next, in the order of selection, with the last taking the place of the first. If only two icons are selected, the effect is that they exchange places.

Undo change to document

ACCESS: Document menu bar: Edit→Undo
              Text tool bar

FUNCTION: Undo the most recent change to a document's content

This menu item takes a variety of forms, depending on the kind of change most recently made to the current document: *Undo Typing, Undo Split, Undo Cut, Undo Paste, Undo Create, Undo Convert, Undo Graphics, Undo Font*, and so forth. Selecting this item causes the recent change to be undone, and toggles this item to a corresponding *Redo (operation)* menu choice. Selecting *Redo* restores the change removed by *Undo*, and redisplays the *Undo* menu choice. The operator can toggle between *Undo* and *Redo* indefinitely.

Undo does not apply to every operation within a document. For example, changing the name of a top-level component, and changing tab fill, are operations that cannot be undone with **Undo**.

Any further editing that modifies the document causes an *Undo* menu choice to be displayed, and the new change becomes the event that can be undone and redone. Thus, the undo capability remembers only one event.

Update container

ACCESS: Desktop menu bar: View→Update
              Desktop pulldown

FUNCTION: Match container's window contents to file system directory

The **Update** menu selection causes the contents (icons) of the current container's window to be updated to reflect files added to, deleted from, or renamed in the corresponding file system directory.

Update expanded link

SELECTION: No

ACCESS: Desktop menu bar: Tools→Admin→Update
FUNCTION: Match expanded link's window contents to original directory

This operation can be used only when the current window displays a link that has been expanded (see page 62). It updates the window's contents to reflect files added to, deleted from, or renamed in the file system directory to which the link initially pointed.

Zoom document

ACCESS: Document menu bar: View→Zoom
FUNCTION: Zoom display of document

This menu item controls the zooming (scaling) of the current document's window. The amount of scaling (zoom factor) is expressed as a percent of full size, with 100% being full size. The window may be zoomed in (more than 100%), to obtain a more detailed look at a smaller amount of material, or zoomed out (less than 100%), to obtain a broad view of a large amount of material. A submenu appears with the following choices:

Toggle	The zoom factor reverts to its previous value
Larger	The zoom factor increases (zoom in)
Smaller	The zoom factor decreases (zoom out)
Percent	A zoom percentage prompt is opened. You can enter the desired zoom factor
Reset	The zoom factor is set to 100.0% (full size)
Page to Window	The zoom factor is adjusted so that a page (or facing pages if facing pages are displayed) is as large as possible without exceeding the width and height of the document's window
Window to Page	The size of the document's window is adjusted so that it displays an entire page (or facing pages if facing pages are displayed), or comes as close as possible, given the size of the screen. The zoom factor is not modified
Window to Frame	The height of the document's window is adjusted to match that of the current frame. There must be an open frame

Graphics
Tool
Palettes

Graphics Tool Palettes

The Tools→Graphics Palettes selection on the document bar Tools pulldown opens a tear-off menu:

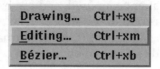

Drawing...	Ctrl+xg
Editing...	Ctrl+xm
Bézier...	Ctrl+xb

The *Drawing* choice opens a graphics drawing palette (see below). *Editing* opens a graphics editing palette (see page 146). *Bezier* opens a graphics Bezier palette (see page 159).

Drawing Tools

The graphics drawing palette consists of icons representing tools and a subedit section:

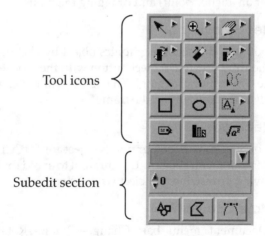

Tool icons {

Subedit section {

Selecting any of the tool icons does not have an immediate effect on any graphics object. The selected icon changes appearance to indicate that that tool is active. The mouse cursor then becomes a tool that you can use to perform various operations.

Many tools have alternate modes, represented by alternate versions of the icon. The icons for these tools have a small black triangle in the upper right corner. If you select this triangle and hold the select button down, a palette showing all the alternate icons for that tool will be opened, and you can select the desired alternative. The chosen alternative will be displayed on the tool palette and will be selected.

◆ **Tip:** Many other tools revert to the selection tool (see page 136) when one operation has completed. If you want to create two lines, for example, you must select the Line tool twice. However, if you select a tool with a double-click of the mouse, the tool will remain selected after being used, and can be used many times in a row. The tool is said to be "sticky." The Active Tool Stickiness Toggle icon in the document menu bar turns the stickiness of the currently selected tool on and off.

Drawing Tools

Select/Size/Move Tool

Also On: Document menu bar: Change→Select/Size/Move Tool

When this is the selected tool, clicking the select mouse button on an object selects the object, making its anchor points visible. The object can then be resized by dragging the anchor points. You can also move the selected object by holding the left mouse button down over the object (not over an anchor point) and dragging the mouse.

Select/Move Tool

With this tool, you can select a graphics object by clicking on it, and move it by holding down the select button with the mouse pointer directly on the object and dragging. The object will not change size or shape; it will only move within the frame.

Select Tool

With this tool, you can select a graphics object for further operations with other tools or menu choices. Use this tool to avoid the risk of accidentally moving or resizing an object while selecting it.

Rotate Circular Tool

Also On: Document menu bar: Change→Rotate→Rotate Circular Tool

The selected object is rotated about its center point, without changing size or shape. If the detent toggle button on the document tool bar is on, the rotation occurs only in amounts of the specified detent angle.

Rotate Magnify Tool

Also On: Document menu bar: Change→Rotate→Rotate Magnify Tool

The object is rotated about the anchor point opposite to the one selected and can be resized, but preserves its proportions. In other words, the ratios of the object's dimensions remain the same as the object is made larger or smaller.

 ### Line Tool

Also On: Document menu bar: Create pulldown

With this tool selected, clicking the select mouse button in the current frame creates a line with one anchor point at the location of the mouse cursor. Holding the select button down, you can move the other end (opposite anchor point) of the line.

 ### Rectangle Tool

Also On: Document menu bar: Create pulldown

With this tool selected, clicking the select mouse button in the current frame creates a rectangle, with one anchor point at the location of the mouse cursor. Holding the select button down, you can move the opposite corner (opposite anchor point) of the rectangle.

 ### Chart Tool

Also On: Document menu bar: Create pulldown

With this tool selected, click the select mouse button in the open frame, and a chart will be created at the cursor location (see page 201). Hold and drag the mouse to size the chart.

 ### Magnify Up Tool

Also On: Document menu bar: View→Magnify→Magnify Up Tool

The mouse cursor becomes a magnifying glass with a plus sign on the lens. Clicking the select mouse button within the current frame causes the display of the frame to zoom in (enlarge).

- **Note:** Zooming changes the printed appearance of the frame as well as the screen display.

- **Note:** The part of the frame under the magnifying glass cursor at the time you click the select button will always be visible after the zoom.

Magnify Down Tool

Also On: Document menu bar: View→Magnify→Magnify Down Tool

- **Note:** Zooming changes the printed appearance of the frame as well as the screen display.

The mouse cursor becomes a magnifying glass with a minus sign on the lens. Clicking the select mouse button within the current frame causes the display of the frame to zoom out (reduce).

 Magnify Reset Command

Also On: Document menu bar: View→Magnify→Reset
Document tool bar

The display of the current frame is reset to normal size, undoing the effect of any previous magnify operations.

↦ Note: The effects of all previous magnifications are undone even if the document has been saved since a zoom up or down.

 Stretch Tool

Also On: Document   menu   bar: Change→Stretch/Shear→Stretch Tool

You must select an object's anchor point to use this tool. The anchor point opposite to the selected one remains fixed in position while you drag the selected anchor point. Unlike the Rotate Magnified tool, this tool changes the object's proportions as you drag the selected anchor.

 Ellipse Tool

Also On: Document menu bar: Create pulldown

With this tool selected, clicking the select mouse button in the current frame creates an ellipse (oval), with one anchor point at the location of the mouse cursor. Holding the select button down, you can move the opposite anchor point, shaping and sizing the ellipse.

Microdocument Tool

Also On: Document menu bar: Create→Text→Microdocument

With this tool selected, clicking the select button in the current frame creates a default microdocument at the position of the mouse cursor. You can type text directly into the microdocument by typing as soon as it is created. You can also open the microdocument by selecting the subedit down arrow on the graphics tool palette (see page 144). Either operation displays the default microcomponent in the component bar, and you can select it and change it to any other component type or change its properties.

◆ Tip: When this tool is visible, whether or not it is selected, and you begin typing in an open frame, a microdocument is created to contain the text you type. See the Text String Tool, below.

Text String Tool

Also On: Document menu bar: Create→Text→Text String

With this tool selected, clicking the select button in the current frame creates a text string at the position of the mouse cursor. You can type text directly into the text string by typing as soon as it is created. An empty text string is indicated by a ⊬ symbol.

◆ **Tip:** When this tool is visible, whether or not it is selected, and you begin typing in an open frame, a text string is created to contain the text you type. See the Microdocument Tool, above.

 Shift Tool

When this tool is active, the mouse cursor becomes a hand. If you move the cursor into the current frame and press the select button, all the contents of the frame will shift in whatever direction you move the mouse as long as you hold the select button down. This may make previously visible frame contents become invisible as they are shifted out of the frame's area on the page.

⊷ **Note:** Shifting affects all the contents of the frame. Grouping is not required. Shifting does not leave the contents grouped if they were not already grouped.

⊷ **Note:** Shifting changes the printed appearance of the frame as well as the screen display.

 Shift Reset Command

Also On: Document tool bar

This command undoes the effects of all previous shifts of the current frame.

⊷ **Note:** The effects of all previous shifts are undone even if the document has been saved since a shift.

 Shear Horizontal Tool

Also On: Document menu bar: Change→Stretch/Shear→Shear Horizontal Tool

A horizontal shear operation may have essentially the same effect as other drag and reshape operations on some objects, such as ellipses or lines. To appreciate the difference, consider a horizontal shear of a rectangle, such as a raster image or a box, oriented so that its edges are parallel to the edges of the frame. If you select the Shear Horizontal tool, then drag an anchor point, the object's horizontal edges will remain parallel to the top and bottom of the frame and will remain the same length. The object will change from a rectangle to a parallelogram.

 ## Shear Vertical Tool

Also On: Document menu bar: Change→Stretch/Shear→Shear Vertical Tool

A vertical shear operation has the same effect as a horizontal shear operation, except for the difference in orientation: if you perform a vertical shear operation on a rectangular object, its vertical edges will remain parallel to the sides of the frame and of fixed length.

 ## Clockwise Arc Tool

Also On: Document menu bar: Create→Arc→Clockwise Arc

This tool allows you to create a clockwise arc: if you press and hold the select button and then move the mouse to the right, an arc will be created with the concave (open) side down; if you move the mouse to the left, the concave side will be up. To resize an arc or change its curvature, use the Select/Size/Move, Stretch, or Rotate Magnified tools.

 ## Counterclockwise Arc Tool

Also On: Document menu bar: Create→Arc→Counterclockwise Arc

This tool allows you to create a counterclockwise arc: if you press and hold the select button and then move the mouse to the left, an arc will be created with the concave (open) side down; if you move the mouse to the right, the concave side will be up.

 ## Freehand Tool

Also On: Document menu bar: Create pulldown

This is identical to the freehand tool on the bezier palette (see page 164).

 ## Named Tool

Also On: Document menu bar: Create pulldown

With this tool selected, click the select mouse button in the open frame, and a named graphics object will be created at the cursor location (see page 166).

Equation Tool

Also On: Document menu bar: Create pulldown

With this tool selected, click the select mouse button in the open frame, and an equation will be created at the cursor location (see page 225).

The CTRL and Shift Keys in Drawing

The CTRL (or Control) and Shift keys have useful effects when drawing some objects. The following table summarizes the effects. An empty cell means that the key makes no difference.

These effects are the same whether drawing is initiated with a tool icon or a menu selection. When you create a poly object, the effects of these keys can be turned on and off by pressing and releasing the keys while creating lines.

Type of Object	Effect of	
	CTRL key	**Shift key**
Line	Diagonal line	Vertical or horizontal line, depending on the initial drag direction
Rectangle	Square	Very narrow rectangle
Ellipse	Circle	
Arc	Quarter circle	
Chart	Square chart	Very narrow chart
Poly	Colinear diagonal line segments	Poly containing only right angles

Creating Named Objects

This part of the drawing palette allows easy selection of masters for components (microdocuments) and named graphics objects to be created. To actually create objects, use the appropriate tools for microdocuments (see page 138) and named graphics objects (see page 140).

Create object
name

Microdocument/
Named graphics
object dialog

If you select the Microdocument tool, and then press the button labeled "Microdocument/Named graphics object dialog" on the graphic above, a *Create Microdocument* dialog box will open:

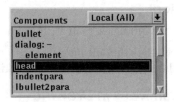

You may highlight any master name on this dialog box, and this name will be displayed in the field labeled "Create object name" on the graphic above. When you use the Microdocument tool to create a microdocument, the selected master will be used.

Similarly, if you select the Named tool, and then press the button labeled "Microdocument/Named graphics object dialog," a *Create Named* dialog box will open. On this dialog box, you can select the master to be used when you create a named graphics object with the Named tool.

Subedit Section

Subedit tools allow you to create and manipulate grouped objects. Graphics objects within a single frame can be associated in arbitrary groups. All kinds of graphics objects, including drawing objects, raster images, microdocuments, text strings, charts, and equations, can be grouped. Groups are themselves graphics objects and may be included in groups. Thus, you can establish hierarchical structures of objects. A given frame can contain an arbitrary number of groups.

The advantage of groups is that they permit you to treat related graphics objects as a single object. For example, suppose that within a frame, you have a raster image of a parts assembly, and a number of part labels. Suppose that each label is to be a microdocument with a box border around it. You could make each combination of microdocument and border a group. Then, you could move each group to its desired position as a unit. As you moved the group, the label and border would stay in the same positions with respect to each other. You would not have to treat the microdocument and border as discrete units unless you wanted to change the properties of the border or the properties or content of the microdocument.

Suppose further that the parts assembly picture and its associated labels are only part of the content of the frame. You could make the image and labels all one group. Then, you could move this group within the frame, and the image and labels would stay in the same positions with respect to each other.

Named graphics objects (see page 166) can be members of groups and can contain groups.

Groups that are directly within the frame (not within other groups) are said to be "top-level groups." Groups that are within other groups are called "nested groups" or "subgroups." The nesting of groups and objects within groups is measured by a number called the "level," or "subedit level." Level zero refers to the top level. Groups at level zero can contain objects (including groups) at level one, and so forth.

To work within a group, select any object that is within the group. This opens the group at the top level. To work within a subgroup, select any object within the subgroup, and then select the subedit level down arrow (or just double-click on the desired object). You cannot reach a nested group without going down the levels from the top level. When you are at a subedit level other than zero, you cannot select any objects not in the current group.

There are only two restrictions:

- A group can contain objects from only one frame, the frame containing the group.

- No object can belong to more than one group, unless one of those groups contains the others. A top-level group is a hierarchy structured like an inverted tree, whose branches are nested groups and whose leaves are graphics objects. Any object is in, at most, one of these hierarchies. The *objects* within the hierarchies may physically overlap within the frame.

Any microdocument within a frame is treated as a group. The upper level of this group is the graphics object itself, which can be selected like any other graphics object and will show anchor points. If you select such an object, and then select the subedit level down arrow, you will enter a subedit of the component within the microdocument, allowing you to change the component's properties and content.

A rectangle is also a group, even though you create it with a single operation using the rectangle tool (see page 137). Polygons and bezier objects are also groups.

You can create or add to groups in the following ways:

- Select any graphics objects, and execute Arrange→Group from the document menu bar. If you have selected top-level objects, a top-level group is created. If you are currently working within a sub-edit, a new subgroup is created at the current level.

- At the top level or within a subedit, select the Create→Group Level or Create→Poly menu choices from the document menu bar or the equivalent tool buttons. Any objects you then create will belong to the new group, until you change subedit level.

- Within a subedit, create any object. It will become a member of the current group.

This is the subedit section of the graphics drawing palette:

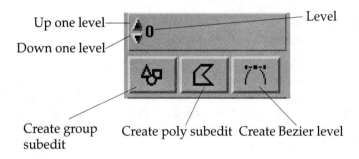

Up one level — Level

Down one level

Create group subedit   Create poly subedit   Create Bezier level

Subedit Level Up/Down

Also On: Document menu bar: Change →Level
          Document tool bar

These up and down arrows allow you to change the current subedit level.

If you select a component within a frame, then select the *down* arrow, the component will be opened for keying and will be listed in the component bar if the component bar is visible.

If you select a group and then select the *down* arrow, the subedit level counter will be incremented, and you can select objects within the group. If you selected a nested group and select *down* again, you can select objects within the nested group. When you reach the level of an individual object, you can select the object for editing. The effect of this depends on the type of object.

The *up* arrow reverses the effect of the down arrow, until the subedit level counter returns to zero.

Create Group Level Command

Also On: Document menu bar: Create pulldown

This command allows you to create a new group at the current subedit level.

The subedit level counter will be incremented. All objects created while this subedit is open (while the level counter is equal to or greater than the value just obtained) will be part of a group. Selecting this command again will create a nested group within this group.

 Create Poly Command

Also On: Document menu bar: Create pulldown

With this command, you can create a new group (a polygon) at the current subedit level.

This command allows you to easily create polygons. The Line tool (see page 137) is automatically selected, and a new subedit is opened (the subedit level counter is incremented). As long as you remain in this subedit, each line you create will automatically begin at the end point of the previous one. The Line tool remains selected when a line is complete, rather than reverting to the Select tool.

The new polygon is a single group, and each line belongs to the group.

 Create Bezier Level Command

Also On: Document menu bar: Create pulldown

This command opens the bezier tool palette (see page 159) with the smooth point tool selected and sticky.

Editing Section

The editing palette contains two parts, command icons and dialog icons:

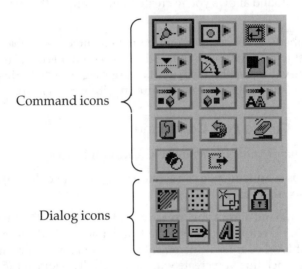

Command icons

Dialog icons

All the icons in the command section take effect on the selected graphics object or objects as soon as you click and release the mouse on the icon. Dialog icons open dialog boxes for operations that use complex options or numeric values.

Command Icons

Many commands have alternate modes, represented by alternate versions of the icon. The icons for these commands have a small black triangle in the upper right corner. If you select this triangle and hold the select button down, a palette showing all the alternate icons for that command will be opened, and you can select the desired alternate. It will take effect immediately, and the selected alternate will be displayed on the tool palette. If no graphics object is selected, the command will have no effect, but you can still select the desired icon to be displayed. Selecting the icon with the mouse pointer not on the small blank triangle causes the displayed icon to take effect without opening a palette of alternates.

Align Centers Command

Also On: Document menu bar: Arrange→Align

All selected objects within the current frame are moved so that their centers are at the same point. Other commands at this point on the palette are:

Align Right Edges

Align Bottom Edges

Align Left Edges

Align Top Edges

Align Left/
Right Centers

Align Top/
Bottom Centers

Align to Frame Center Command

Also On: Document menu bar: Arrange→Align to Frame

All selected objects are moved so that they are centered within the current open frame. If multiple objects are selected, they are *not* moved as a group. They are each centered individually, with the result that they will overlap. Other commands at this point on the palette are:

Align to Frame Right
Edge

Align to Frame
Bottom Edge

Align to Frame Left
Edge

Align to Frame Top
Edge

Align to Frame
Left/Right Center

Align to Frame
Top/Bottom Center

Size to Frame All Command

Also On: Document menu bar: Change→Size to Frame

The selected object is resized so that its horizontal and vertical dimensions match those of the frame, and the object is centered within the frame. Microdocuments do not change size but are centered. If multiple objects are selected, they *are* resized and centered as a group. Note that if an object is bigger than the frame, it will be reduced. An object may be reduced in one dimension and increased in another. Proportions are *not* preserved. Other commands at this point on the palette are:

Size to Frame Vertical
The selected objects are resized in the vertical dimension only. Proportions are *not* preserved.

Size to Frame Horizontal
The selected objects are resized in the horizontal dimension only. Proportions are *not* preserved.

Size to Frame Diagonal
The selected objects are resized in both horizontal and vertical dimensions until the objects match the frame in at least one dimension. Proportions *are* preserved.

Flip Vertical Command

Also On: Document menu bar: Change→Flip

The selected object is flipped (mirrored) around a horizontal axis running through the center of the object. If multiple objects are selected, they are flipped as a group. Other commands at this point on the palette are:

 Flip Horizontal
The selected object is flipped (mirrored) around a vertical axis running through the center of the object.

 Flip Diagonal
The selected object is flipped (mirrored) around an axis running from the lower left to the upper right control points of the object.

 Rotate Clockwise by Detent Command

Also On: Document menu bar: Change→Rotate→Clockwise

The selected object is rotated about its center in a clockwise direction. The angle through which the object is rotated is determined by the current detent, set either on the *Graphics Tool Palette Animation* dialog box (see page 155) or the document tool bar. A negative detent causes rotation in a counterclockwise direction.

If several objects are selected, they are rotated about their common center as though they were grouped.

 Rotate Counterclockwise by Detent Command

Also On: Document menu bar: Change→Rotate→Counterclockwise

This works the same way as the Rotate Clockwise by Detent command, except that rotation is in the opposite direction.

 Front Command

Also On: Document menu bar: Arrange→Move to Front

The selected object is brought to the front of the diagram (it obscures any overlapping objects). If more than one object is selected, they are put in front of all other objects, without changing the front to back relationships among the selected objects.

 Back Command

Also On: Document menu bar: Arrange→Move to Back

The selected object is put to the back of the diagram (it is obscured by any overlapping objects). If more than one object is selected, they are put behind all other objects, without changing the front to back relationships among the selected objects.

Convert to Iso Left Command

Also On: Document menu bar: Change→Convert→to Iso

Convert a two-dimensional object to a three-dimensional object by projecting it onto the left (Y-Z) isometric plane.

Convert to Iso Top Command

Also On: Document menu bar: Change→Convert→to Iso

Convert a two-dimensional object to a three-dimensional object by projecting it onto the top (Z-X) isometric plane.

Convert to Iso Right Command

Also On: Document menu bar: Change→Convert→to Iso

Convert a two-dimensional object to a three-dimensional object by projecting it onto the right (X-Y) isometric plane.

Convert from Iso Left Command

Also On: Document menu bar: Change →Convert→from Iso

Convert a three-dimensional object to a two-dimensional object by reversing the effect of a Convert to Iso Left command.

Convert from Iso Top Command

Also On: Document menu bar: Change →Convert→from Iso

Convert a three-dimensional object to a two-dimensional object by reversing the effect of a Convert to Iso Top command.

Convert from Iso Right Command

Also On: Document menu bar: Change →Convert→from Iso

Convert a three-dimensional object to a two-dimensional object by reversing the effect of a Convert to Iso Right command.

Convert to Outline Command

Also On: Document menu bar: Change →Convert

Selected text is converted to outline form. The text ceases to have text properties and becomes a group of outline objects, one object for each character (it is no longer within a microdocument).

◆ **Tip:** Converting text to outline allows graphics manipulations such as stretching and flipping to be performed.

Convert to Poly Command

Also On: Document menu bar: Cha_n_ge →_C_onvert

Connected selected objects such as lines, arcs, or outline objects are converted to polys.

Group Command

Also On: Document menu bar: _A_rrange pulldown

All selected objects are placed in a group. If any of the selected objects are already groups, they are nested within the new group, that is, they are at a lower subedit level.

Ungroup Command

Also On: Document menu bar: _A_rrange pulldown

Groups in the current selection at the current subedit level are ungrouped.

◆ **Tip:** If the subedit level is greater than zero, the newly ungrouped objects continue to be part of the next higher level group. If any of the newly ungrouped objects are themselves groups (at a lower subedit level), these groups are not ungrouped. Ungrouping takes place only at the current subedit level.

Undo Command

Also On: Document menu bar: _E_dit pulldown

The most recent graphics operation is undone.

•◦ **Note:** This command will not work after the frame is closed.

Redo Command

Also On: Document menu bar: _E_dit pulldown

Any graphics operation that has just been undone with the _Undo_ command is put back into effect.

•◦ **Note:** This command will not work after the frame is closed.

Delete Command

All selected objects are deleted.

↔ **Note:** The objects are not cut to the clipboard and can be retrieved only by immediately executing an *Undo* command without closing the frame and without performing any other graphics operation.

Duplicate Command

When you click on this command, all selected objects in the current frame are duplicated. The original objects do not move, but duplicates are created in the same positions as the selected objects. You can select and drag each duplicate to a new location.

◆ **Tip:** If you drag the duplicate by an anchor point, the opposite anchor point will remain in place. The duplicate will stretch and rotate but will continue to share an anchor point with the original. If your intent is to create an object the same size and shape as the original and move it away, select part of the object itself, not an anchor point.

Close Frame Command

Also On: Document menu bar: Change pulldown

The currently open frame is closed.

Dialog Section

Each of the icons in the dialog section causes a dialog box to open. Only one of these dialog boxes can be open at a time for a given document. If you open one and then open another, the second one replaces the first. In many cases, information in the fields on these dialog boxes is remembered from one use to another as long as the document is open, so if you return to a dialog box, you can take up where you left off.

In the upper left corner of each of these dialog boxes, there are seven icons, matching the dialog icons on the editing palette. These enable you to shift among these seven dialog boxes.

In the upper right corner are two icons. The right-most one is always a symbol indicating the type of graphics object that is selected. The following symbols are used if there is no selection or more than one object is selected:

No selection: Ø   Multiple objects:

The icon to the left of the type indicator shows the current graphics tool.

Fill/Edge Dialog

Also On: Document menu bar: Cha_n_ge pulldown

A *Fill/Edge* dialog box opens:

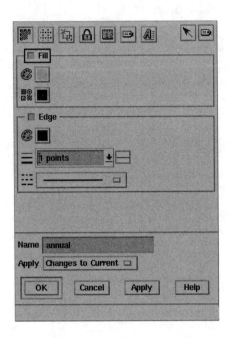

The **Fill** section contains a color indicator (next to the color palette icon) that shows the current fill color. The pattern indicator immediately below shows a sample of the current fill pattern. The **Edge** section contains a color indicator showing the current edge color.

- **Note:** Fill and edge properties apply to objects whose edges are distinct objects, such as lines and curves. For example, you can assign fill and edge properties to a rectangle, arc, or ellipse, but not to a raster image or component.

- **Tip:** You can select several objects and apply fill and edge properties to them as though they were grouped, but doing so does not group them. For example, if two overlapping arcs enclose an area, you can select both arcs and adjust the fill of the area.

- **Note:** The color and pattern indicator squares in this dialog box may display a ? instead of a current setting. This will happen if you select two objects with different fill or edge properties. It will also happen if a particular property does not apply to a selected object.

∞ **Note:** The settings currently displayed on this dialog box will be the initial values for new unnamed graphics objects you create, as long as you select **Apply** after making any changes.

◆ **Tip:** You can create your own patterns (see page 181) and colors (see page 173).

The **Fill** group controls the fill of the selected object. Selecting the color indicator brings up a palette of available colors. The pattern indicator brings up a palette of patterns. The interior of the object is filled with the selected pattern in the selected color. Selecting the solid black square for the pattern causes the entire interior of the object to be filled with the selected color.

The button labeled **Fill** controls whether or not the object's fill is actually drawn. If it is drawn, the object will obscure any object behind it, no matter what the color or pattern of the fill. If it is not drawn, objects beneath the selected one are visible through it.

The **Edge** group controls the edges of the selected object. Selecting the color indicator brings up a palette of available colors. The pulldown beneath the color indicator brings up a list of line weights (thicknesses). You can enter a new numeric value in the field associated with the weight pulldown, and the new weight will be added to the pulldown for objects within the current document. The second pulldown allows you to choose from among various edge patterns, including a solid edge.

The **Name** field is read-only and contains the object's name if the object is a named graphics object.

Grid Dialog

Also On: Document menu bar: Change→Frame Settings→Grid

A *Grid* dialog box opens:

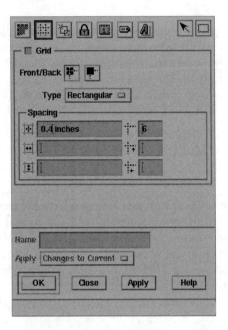

The grid is composed of *grid lines* that are demarcated by dots when the grid is visible. The distance between grid lines defines a *major unit*, and the distance between dots defines a *minor unit*. The function of the grid is to facilitate alignment and sizing of graphics objects: when **Grid Align** is on (see page 155), any active anchor point that is dragged snaps to a nearby grid point when the select button is released.

The **Grid** button controls visibility of the grid. The **Front** and **Back** buttons determine whether the visible grid is displayed as though it were in front of or behind all the objects in the frame. With the Type pulldown you can choose *Rectangular* (two dimensional) or *Isometric* (three dimensional).

The **Spacing** group allows you to set the sizes of the major and minor grid units. For a rectangular grid, this group contains three combination fields. In each combination field, the left-hand field contains the major grid unit. The right-hand field contains the number of minor units in a major unit. The smaller the left value and the larger the right number, the finer the grid will be. You can use the first of the three combination fields to set both horizontal and vertical grid spacing. Or, you can use the second field to set horizontal spacing and the third to set vertical spacing.

If you enter identical values in the second and third fields, these fields will be cleared and the values transferred to the first field, since you have made the spacing the same in both dimensions.

If the grid is isometric, the spacing is the same in all dimensions, and only one combination field is displayed.

 **Animation Dialog**

Also On: Document menu bar: Change→Frame Settings→Animation

An *Animation* dialog box opens:

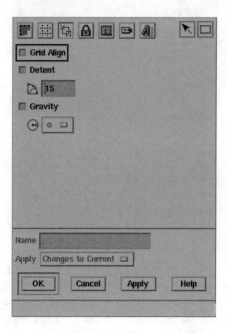

The **Grid Align** button controls whether or not anchor points that are dragged must snap to a grid position.   **Detent** defines the angle through which an object is rotated by the Rotate Clockwise by Detent and Rotate Counterclockwise by Detent commands.

If **Gravity** is on, and an anchor is dragged and released near an anchor point of another object, the dragged anchor point will snap to the position of the nearby anchor point. This is useful in adjustments such as making sure that the ends of line segments meet. The associated pulldown palette of circles determines how close the moving anchor point must be to another anchor point for gravity to take effect. The smaller the circle selected, the closer they must be.

Locks Dialog

Also On: Document menu bar: Cha<u>ng</u>e pulldown

A *Locks* dialog box opens:

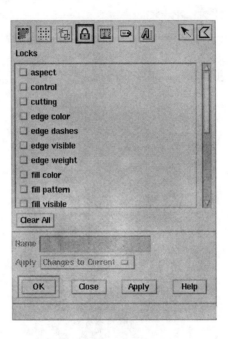

Lock settings are listed in the **Locks** slider and can be set and cleared by pressing the toggle buttons to the left of the descriptions. The **Clear All** button clears all at once. If two objects are selected that have conflicting settings for some locks, the buttons for those locks will be shown with fuzzy outlines. Pressing a fuzzy button turns the lock on for all selected objects.

The **Name** field is read-only, and contains the object's name if the object is a named graphics object.

Measurements Dialog

Also On: Document menu bar: Cha_nge pulldown

A *Measurements* dialog box opens:

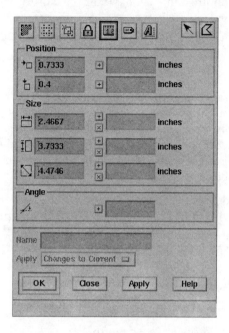

This dialog box lets you adjust the size, position, and rotation of an object by entering numeric values.

The **Position** group displays the current horizontal and vertical position of the selected object's leftmost and uppermost points, respectively. The upper left corner of the frame has horizontal and vertical coordinates of zero, and increasing positive coordinates indicate positions down and to the right. You can directly enter new values in these fields. Or, you can select the + signs to the right of these fields to open the position increment fields. You can then enter increments (which may be negative) for the horizontal or vertical positions, or both. Each time you press the **Apply** button, the object's position will be incremented by the specified amounts.

The **Size** group displays the object's current dimensions: horizontal, vertical, and diagonal. You can directly enter new horizontal and vertical dimensions or a new diagonal measurement. Or, you can select the + signs to the right of these fields to open the size increment fields. If you enter values in the increment fields, then each time you press

Apply, the corresponding dimension is incremented by the value in the increment field (which may be negative). Finally, you can select the **x** signs to the right of these fields to open the size multiplier fields. If you enter values in the multiplier fields, then each time you press **Apply**, the corresponding dimension is multiplied by the value in the multiplier field. A value less than one reduces the size of the object.

You can use the horizontal and vertical size fields together or separately, or you can use the last pair of fields in the **Size** group to size diagonally.

◆ **Tip:** If several objects are selected, they can be repositioned and resized as though they were grouped. Position changes affect all of them equally, so they stay in the same positions with respect to each other. Size changes are distributed among the objects along with proportional changes in the distance between them, so that the set of objects changes size.

The **Angle** field specifies a rotation angle in degrees. Positive values indicate clockwise motion. Each time you press **Apply**, the selected objects are rotated by the specified amount. If several objects are selected, they are all rotated as a group around a common center.

Name Dialog

Also On: Document menu bar: Change pulldown

A *Name* dialog box opens (see page 167).

Text Dialog

Also On: Document menu bar: Change→Frame Settings→Text Defaults

A *Text* dialog box opens:

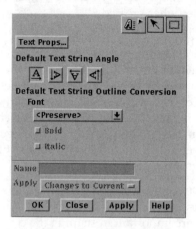

The **Text Props** button opens a **Text Properties** dialog box (see page 129). You can change the frame's default font.

The four radio buttons in the **Default Text Angle** group specify the rotation of newly created text strings. The left button, with a horizontal arrow pointing to the right, is the setting for horizontal, right side up text, running from left to right.

The Default Text String Outline Conversion Font pulldown and associated **Bold** and **Italic** buttons allow you to choose a font for converting text strings to outline form.

Bezier Curves

This section will first discuss bezier curves and how they are shaped, and will then discuss the specific tools available for creating and shaping them.

Bezier Objects

A *bezier object* is a graphic object that consists of *bezier points* and *bezier curve objects*. A bezier point is a single point that helps to define a bezier curve. A bezier curve object (or *segment*) is a smooth curve that runs between two bezier points. A bezier curve is composed of one or more segments. Bezier curves can be stretched and resized and will retain their smoothness as they change shape.

∞ Note: Splines created in Interleaf 5 are converted to bezier objects in Interleaf 6 when you select them for editing.

The shape of the curve at a point that joins two segments may be smooth or it may be a sharp corner. Bezier points may be smooth points (producing smooth curves when created) or corner points (producing straight lines when created).

Bezier objects are groups (see page 142). Within a group, each curve segment, or bezier curve (the part of the object between two adjacent points) is an element of the group. When you create or edit a bezier object, you enter a subedit of the group. If you delete bezier curves from a bezier object such that the object is cut into two unconnected parts, you can immediately reconnect the two objects by connecting any pair of unconnected points. However, if you go to a higher level (lower subedit level number) with the two parts still separated, they become separate groups.

A bezier point has two associated *tangent lines*. One tangent line is tangent to each curve segment attached to the point. The angle and direction of these lines are important in shaping the curve. You can rotate a tangent line by dragging an endpoint. The curve will change shape to remain tangent to the line. By rotating the tangent line over the curve, you can reverse the concavity of the curve. You can also change the length of a tangent line by dragging an endpoint. The longer the line, the flatter the curve will be at that point. Tangent lines become visible when the bezier point to which they are attached is selected.

Dragging a bezier point does not change the length or angle of tangent lines. Shaping a curve by dragging a point on the curve can do so, and you can select the endpoint of a tangent line away from the bezier point and drag the endpoint.

If you cut a bezier point that is an endpoint (has only one attached curve), the attached curve will vanish. If you cut a bezier point that is connected to two other bezier points, the two curves attached to it will be replaced by a single curve, and the shape of that curve will be determined by the tangent lines of the remaining bezier points.

Within an open frame, you can create bezier points. For the first point, this automatically increments the subedit level counter. Points created in succession will belong to the same subedit level (the same group). As you continue to create points without interruption, these points will be joined by bezier curve objects (you must leave each point selected as you create the next). You can also create bezier curves by freehand drawing. When you do this, Interleaf 6 creates bezier points and adjusts tangent lines to match the shape you draw.

When you create a bezier smooth point (other than by freehand draw-ing), you drag the mouse to establish the initial direction and length of its tangent lines. The new point and its tangent lines become visible when you start to drag while holding down the select button. If you press the CTRL key while dragging, the tangent lines will always be a diagonal, 45 degrees from horizontal, running from upper left to lower right. If you press the SHIFT key while dragging, the lines will always be horizontal.

You can adjust the shapes of existing curves by rotating and changing the length of tangent lines, straightening curves, dragging a point on a curve, and dragging the bezier points.

Tangent lines associated with bezier curves that have been straight-ened do not appear when the points are selected. They will reappear if the curves are shaped into a non-linear shape. The same is true of curves that are straight because they were created between two corner points.

Bezier objects, like other graphics objects, also have anchor points, which are visible when the object is selected at its top level (before en-tering a subedit). Dragging an anchor point affects the shape of the bezier curves, but gives you less control than entering a subedit and using the bezier tools.

Some examples of bezier operations:

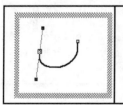

A bezier curve segment connects two bezier smooth points. The point on the left is se-lected and its tangent lines are displayed.

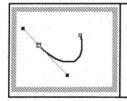

The same curve has been modified by mov-ing the endpoint of the lower tangent line to the right. The upper tangent line has no cur-rent significance since no curve is connected to this point adjacent to that line.

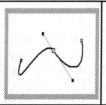

A new point has been added on the left, and connected to the previously selected point. This adds a new segment to the bezier object.

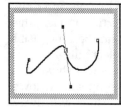

The same tangent line endpoint has been moved to the left, moving both tangent lines and changing the shape of both curve segments.

By default, the tangent angle at a bezier point is locked. This means that when one tangent line at a point is rotated, the other line also rotates. If you unlock the angle, you can rotate one line without affecting the other:

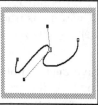

The lower tangent line's endpoint has been moved further to the left, while the other line has remained in place. The curve segment to the right of this point has changed shape, while the segment to the left is unchanged.

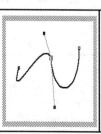

With tangent angles still unlocked, a point near the middle of the curve segment on the right has been dragged downward. The upper tangent line and curve segment on the left are unchanged, while the lower tangent line has rotated and lengthened to match the new shape of the curve.

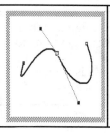

With the tangent angle locked again, a point near the middle of the curve segment on the right has been dragged to the right. Both curve segments have changed shape, and both tangent lines have moved.

◆ **Tip:** Any change to a tangent line angle of a bezier point will cause a change to all curves connected to that point through points with locked tangent angles. If you want to reshape part of a bezier object without affecting other parts, isolate the part to be changed by unlocking tangent angles.

Bezier Tools

 Select/Size/Move Tool

Also On: Document menu bar: Change→Select/Size/Move Tool

When this is the selected tool, clicking the select mouse button on an object selects the object. You can change the shape of a selected bezier object by dragging a bezier point, dragging a curve segment, or dragging the movable end of a tangent line.

 Select/Move Tool

Also On: Document menu bar: Arrange→Select/Move Tool

With this tool, you can select a graphics object by clicking on it. You can change the shape of a selected bezier object by dragging a bezier point or dragging (shaping) a curve segment, but you cannot rotate or change the length of a tangent line.

 Select Tool

Also On: Document menu bar: Arrange→Select Tool

With this tool, you can select a graphics object for further operations with other tools or menu choices. You can select a bezier object or points or curves within it, but you cannot move the object or its points or change its tangent lines.

 Shape Tool

Also On: Document menu bar: Change→Bezier

With this tool selected, you can press and hold the select button over any point on a bezier curve, and drag that point, reshaping the curve. Curves connected to the point being dragged through bezier points with tangent angles locked will also change shape, if your change rotates the tangent lines adjacent to the curve containing the moving point.

 Connect Command

Also On: Document menu bar: Change→Bezier

You can choose two bezier points, then join them with a bezier curve by selecting this command. The two points must be in the same bezier object, or you cannot select them at the same time. Also, each one must have no more than one curve attached to it. This command is useful for closing a loop of successively created bezier objects. If you select just one endpoint of an open loop and then execute this command, that endpoint will automatically be joined to the other endpoint.

Smooth Point Tool

Also On: Document menu bar: Create→Bezier

With this tool selected, clicking the select button creates a bezier smooth point.

Corner Point Tool

Also On: Document menu bar: Create→Bezier

With this tool selected, clicking the select button creates a bezier corner point.

Split Tool

Also On: Document menu bar: Change→Bezier

With this tool selected, if you click the select button over a bezier curve, a bezier point will be created at that point, dividing the curve into two bezier curves. The curve on which you click must be within an open subedit.

Straighten Command

Also On: Document menu bar: Change→Bezier

When you select this command, all selected bezier curves become straight lines. If you are in a subedit of a bezier object and nothing is selected, all curves in that object become straight lines.

Freehand Tool

Also On: Document menu bar: Create→Freehand
            Graphics drawing palette

This tool turns the mouse into a drawing pen. With this tool selected, move the mouse cursor to the desired beginning point, press the left button, and move the mouse in any direction to create a freehand drawing. The drawing operation stops when you release the mouse button. Each operation creates a single graphics object (a Bezier object), consisting of as many bezier curves as necessary to create the desired shape. This bezier object may then be moved, stretched, sized, and rotated using the other bezier tools.

Unlock Angles Command

Also On: Document menu bar: Cha_nge→_Bezier

This command unlocks the tangent angle at the selected bezier point.

 Lock Angles Command

Also On: Document menu bar: Cha_nge→_Bezier

This command locks the tangent angle at the selected bezier point.

Rotate Circular and Rotate Magnify Tools

The Rotate Circular (see page 136) and Rotate Magnify (see page 136) tools on the graphics drawing palette are useful in editing bezier objects.

With the Rotate Circular tool selected, you can select a bezier point and drag and rotate one of its tangent lines. Both tangent lines will rotate by the same amount, even if the angle is unlocked, so that the angle between them remains fixed, but neither tangent line will change length.

With the Rotate Circular tool, you can select a bezier curve segment, so that its anchor points appear, and rotate the curve by dragging its anchor points. The curve will rotate about a center point halfway between its endpoints, and will not change shape. The curves adjacent to it at either end will change shape and remain connected. If you select several adjacent curve segments, you can rotate them as a group around a center point determined by all their endpoints. The group of curves will not change shape and will remain fixed in relation to each other; curves adjacent to the group at either end will change shape. If you select two curves that are both adjacent to a single curve between them, the selected curve and the one between will rotate as a group. Or, you can select two curves separated by more than one curve. The curves will rotate as a group and attached curves will change shape. If you select all, or all but one, of the curves in a bezier object, and rotate circular, the entire bezier object will rotate. None of its curves will change shape, and all will remain in the same position in relation to each other.

With the Rotate Magnify tool, you can drag the endpoint of a tangent line and both rotate and resize the line. This tool (unlike the Select/ Size/Move tool) will always rotate both tangent lines at that point by the same amount, even if the angle is unlocked. Both lines will be resized symmetrically.

Using the Rotate Magnify tool to rotate bezier curve objects is similar to using the Rotate Circular tool in the way selected curves are grouped and the way attached curves reshape to remain attached. However, instead of rotating about a center point determined by the bezier points selected, the selected curve(s) rotate about the selected bezier point most nearly opposite the selected anchor point. The selected curves maintain their shape, but can change in size as well as rotation. If you select all the curves in the object, you can rotate and resize the object while preserving all its proportions.

Named Graphics Objects

Named graphics objects give you a way to create named masters of graphics objects, just as masters of components and frames have names. As with other masters, you can set the properties of each master, create instances of it, and so on.

Named graphics objects, like other named objects, can be exported from catalogs.

Since groups can be named graphics objects, and named graphics objects can contain groups or other named graphics objects, you can create arbitrarily complex named graphics objects. This can be quite helpful when you wish to create many graphics objects whose contents are identical or similar. Unless a named graphics object's master is under catalog control, you can modify its properties or content.

To create a named graphics object from an existing master, use the Named tool on the graphics drawing palette (see page 140). You can select the master using the drawing palette (see page 141). The Create→Named choice on the document menu bar provides equivalent functions.

To define a new named graphics object master, select any graphics object, and then select Change→Name on the document menu bar. This opens a *Name* dialog box (see page 167). Press the **New** button on the *Name* dialog box. A *Define Graphics Master* dialog box opens:

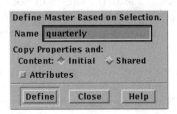

Enter the name the new master is to have in the **Name** field, and press the **Define** button. The **Initial** and **Shared** radio buttons specify whether or not the shared–content setting is on for subsequently created instances. If you select **Initial**, each instance is a one-time snapshot of the master, after which any changes to the master's content have no effect on the instance. If you select **Shared**, each instance is a continuous "link" to the master's content, with the important distinction that each shared instance can have its own transformation (including size) and active set of fill and edge properties. As with all settings on the master, regardless of the master's shared setting, each instance can have its shared setting changed to the opposite.

The **Attributes** button determines whether or not the attributes of the graphics selection (if that selection is named and has been assigned attribute values) are copied to the new master.

The Properties Dialog Box for Named graphics Objects

The *Name* dialog box, which is the interface to the properties of named graphics objects, can be accessed with Change→Name on the document menu bar, or by selecting the Name Dialog icon (see page 158) on the graphics editing palette dialog section.

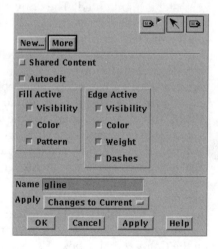

Use the **New** button to create a new master (see page 166). The **More** button lists the usual options, plus three options specific to named graphics objects:

Revert to Master Size/Rotation	If a shared-content instance has been sized, rotated, sheared, or stretched, this menu choice restores it to the size and rotation of the master.
Convert to Named	This menu choice allows you to convert one or more graphics objects to a named graphics object. This includes changing a named graphics object into an instance of another master. A *Convert* dialog box opens:

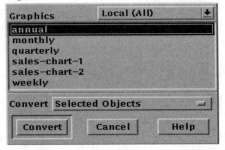

The **Convert** button effects the conversion of one or more objects to named graphics objects of whichever master is highlighted. The Convert pulldown has three choices. If you select *Selected Objects*, each currently selected graphics object is converted to a named graphics object of the specified name. If there are multiple objects selected, each one becomes a separate named graphics object. If you select *Selected Objects as Group*, all currently selected graphics object are grouped, and the resulting group is converted to a named graphics object of the specified name. Only one named graphics object is created on each operation, no matter how many objects are selected. If you select *All Instances*, all instances (in the current document) of the same master as the selected instance, are converted to named graphics objects, with the name highlighted on the *Convert* dialog box. *All Instances* can only be executed when there is exactly one graphics object selected, and that object is a named graphics object.

Convert to Unnamed	This menu choice converts named graphics objects to unnamed objects. There is a submenu with two options. *Selected* converts all currently selected named graphics objects to unnamed objects. The *All* menu choice can only be executed when there is exactly one graphics object selected, and that object is a named graphics object. All instances (in the current document) of the same master as the selected instance, are converted to unnamed objects.

On the properties dialog box for named graphics objects (see page 167), the **Shared Content** button determines whether or not an instance of a named graphics object shares content with the master. If **Autoedit** is on, selecting an object within the named graphics object opens an appropriate editor for that object, without an extra step to go from the subedit to the object's editor.

For the **Fill Active** and **Edit Active** areas of the *Name* dialog box, see the following section.

The Fill Active and Edit Active Buttons

The **Fill Active** and **Edit Active** areas of the *Name* dialog box enable you to control the transfer of fill and edge properties between instances and between masters and instances. The effect is to allow instances to have different fill and edge properties than masters, even when shared content is in effect, when desired.

The **Fill Active** group contains three toggle buttons, applying to the visibility, color, and pattern of the named graphics object's fill. The **Edit Active** group contains four buttons, applying to the visibility, color, weight (thickness), and dash pattern of the object. Each of these seven buttons corresponds to a property that can be set on the *Fill/ Edge* dialog box (see page 152). The functioning of these buttons is discussed in more detail below, but in general, their function is as follows: if a given button is on, the corresponding property is copied from this instance to other instances or the master during various operations, and the property defined for this object overrides the master property even when content is shared. If a button is off, the same operations do not copy properties from this instance to other instances or the master, and if this instance shares content, the master's property overrides the property defined for this instance.

Changing any of these properties on the *Fill/Edge* dialog box of an instance causes the corresponding **Active** button to be turned on for that instance, if it was not already on.

Suppose you have several instances of one master named graphics object. If you select one instance, open a *Fill/Edge* dialog box, and apply *All Props to All*, only those fill and edge properties for which the **Active** button is on will be copied to the other instances and to the master.

◆ **Tip:** Since changing a fill/edge property immediately turns on the corresponding **Active** button, if you make a change, and then immediately apply All Props to All, the change will always be propagated to other instances. This will not happen if you turn off the **Active** button before applying All Props to All.

∞ **Note:** Because changing a fill/edge property turns on the corresponding **Active** button, the **Active** buttons do not change the effect of applying All Changes to All on the *Fill/Edge* dialog box.

If a named graphics object shares content, then the instance inherits from the master all fill/edge properties for which the **Active** button is off on the instance. If you change a property on the instance's *Fill/Edge* dialog box, the corresponding Active button is turned on, and the change you have just made overrides the master's property for this instance. If you go to the instance's *Name* dialog box, and turn off the **Active** button for that property, the instance will again inherit the property from the master. If you then turn the **Active** button on, the change that you had made once again overrides the master's property. This is true even if you save, close, and reopen the document before you turn the **Active** button on again.

Whether or not an instance of a named graphics object shares content, the **Active** buttons control updating the master's properties from that instance's *Name* dialog box. If you select *Update Master Props* from the More pulldown on the instance's *Name* dialog box, only those fill/ edge properties for which the instance has the **Active** button turned on will be propagated to the master.

If a master named graphics object specifies shared content, and you convert a graphics object to be an instance of that named graphics object (see page 168), all fill/edge properties of the master are inherited by the instance. However, if the master does not have the **Shared Content** button on, then the **Active** buttons on the master's *Name* dialog box determine which fill/edge properties of the master override the properties already set on the instance that is being converted.

The **Active** buttons on the master's *Name* dialog box also control the propagation of the master's fill/edge properties to any instance when you execute *Revert to Master Props* on the More pulldown of the instance's *Name* dialog box. Any fill/edge property of the master for which the master's **Active** button is off will not override the corresponding property of the instance; the state of the instance's **Active** button does not matter.

Color
Palette

Color Palette

The color palette permits you to change and delete the definitions of existing colors and to define new colors. Your changes to the color palette apply only to the current document, and to any document created later as a copy of it.

You can copy colors to create new ones, and you can cut or copy colors and paste them between documents. Changes to the color palette take effect in the *Color* dialog boxes for graphics fills and edges, text, and components, when you select File→Apply on the *Color Palette Editor* dialog box.

⇨ **Note:** Colors are not exported from catalogs.

◆ **Tip:** A color that is cut or copied from a *Color Palette Editor* dialog box is placed on the clipboard as a "palette" icon and can be pasted directly onto the desktop. If you select and open this icon, you will see a *Color Palette Editor* dialog box containing only that color. You may modify the color, save and close the dialog box, and paste the icon into a *Color Palette Editor* dialog box. A "palette" icon looks like this:

The color palette may be opened during operations that involve the colors of specific objects, such as color editing in images or charts. In these cases, you may make changes that apply only to the object being edited. The *Color Palette Editor* dialog box may not appear, but the *Color Editor* dialog box described below under "Modifying colors" will be available.

A *Color Palette Editor* dialog box is opened:

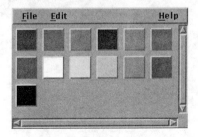

Creating and Deleting Colors

All existing color definitions for the current document are displayed in the rows of squares. Any color may be selected for editing; selection causes the square to increase in size. To create a new color, copy and modify an existing one.

You can select a color and then execute Edit→Cut to remove it or Edit→Copy to copy it. A cut or copied definition can be pasted in this or another color palette by using one of the four options on the Edit→Paste submenu:

Edit→Paste→Before	This choice requires that a color be selected in the destination palette. The pasted color is positioned immediately before the selected color.
Edit→Paste→After	This choice requires that a color be selected in the destination palette. The pasted color is positioned immediately after the selected color.
Edit→Paste→Beginning	The pasted color is positioned at the beginning (upper left) of the rows of colors.
Edit→Paste→End	The pasted color is positioned at the end (lower right) of the rows of colors.

Modifying Colors

To modify a color, double-click on it, or click on it and select Edit→Open. The selected color's *Color Editor* dialog box appears:

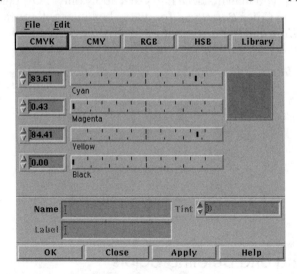

Move the sliders to vary the different components of the color. The sample color square in the upper right corner of the dialog box shows the current value of the color in the upper half of the square and the value specified by the sliders in the lower half. When you select **Apply**, the value specified by the sliders becomes current and fills the entire square. You can use the up/down arrow fields to the left of the sliders to make entries with higher precision than the sliders permit.

The top row of radio buttons allows you to select **CMYK** (Cyan–Magenta–Yellow–Black), **CMY** (Cyan–Magenta–Yellow), **RGB** (Red–Green–Blue), and **HSB** (Hue–Saturation–Brightness) color models. The sliders are updated to correspond to each change. The color remains the same. You can also select **Library**, to access a color library (see page 176).

Apply or **OK** apply your changes (you must execute File→Save from the *Palette Editor* dialog box and save the document to make them permanent).

Edit→Complement turns the color into its complementary color. Edit→Dilute allows you to modify the color by diluting it with a specified amount of white or black. Edit→Undo and Edit→Redo allow you to undo and redo the most recent change. File→Revert to→Saved undoes all changes since the last **Apply**. File→Revert to→Backup undoes all changes since the second preceding **Apply**.

The up/down arrow **Tint** field allows you to lighten or darken a selected color.

◆ **Tip:** A color must be named before you can adjust the tint or assign a label.

◆ **Tip:** If you type in a tint value, and then select Apply, the displayed color in the lower half of the sample color square will be adjusted to the specified tint and then made current. If you click on the background of the dialog box instead, the current color will be adjusted to the specified tint and the result will be displayed in the lower half of the sample color square; the current color, displayed in the upper half of the sample color square, will not be changed.

If you are modifying a gray scale image, you will not see the sliders for different colors and you cannot select different color models. You will see a single slider ranging from pure white to pure black, and you can choose the desired shade of gray.

Named and Labeled Colors

You can *name* colors, which gives you an easy way to select a particular color when applying colors to graphics fills or edges (see page 152) or to text (see page 129). Colors selected from a library (see page 176) are already named. You can also *label* a combination of a named color and a tint value.

Modifying the Color Palette

Edit→Undo undoes the most recent change. Edit→Redo reverses the most recent Undo. If you make changes using the *Color Palette Editor* dialog box and the Color Editor File→Save menu choice, *all* those changes made with the color editor are undone and redone as one change.

File→Save on the *Color Palette Editor* dialog box applies all changes; they are made permanent when you save the document. File→Apply makes changes available for setting the fill and edge colors of graphics objects (see page 152).

File→Save As allows you to save the entire palette as a separate desktop icon. A *Save As* dialog box opens:

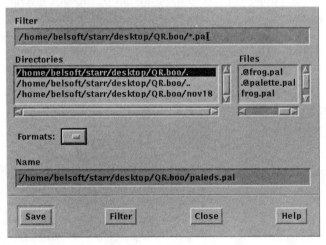

This dialog box, which operates as a *File Selection* dialog box (see page 116), has a **Save** button to save the color palette. There is no choice of formats. You can change the path in the **Name** field.

Once you execute File→Save As, you can copy and paste the resulting desktop icon into a *Color Palette Editor* dialog box, adding all the saved colors to the open palette.

Color Libraries

A color library is a range of pre-specified colors. By using a library, you can maintain conformance with a specific color standard.

When you select the **Library** radio button, the *Color Editor* dialog box changes to this appearance:

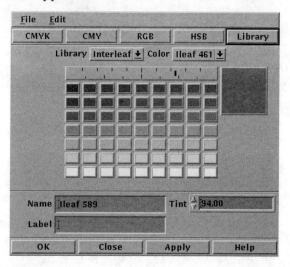

The **Library** pulldown allows you to select from the available libraries. The *Interleaf* library is standard with Interleaf 6. Within a library, the **Color** pulldown allows you to select a specific named color.

The array of seven rows of nine squares each displays a part of the range of colors in the current library. These squares are sequential within the library, running from the upper left, down columns, across to the lower right. The slider above this array controls the part of the library that is currently displayed. Move the slider until the desired range of colors is displayed, then select any displayed square. The name of the selected color is displayed in the **Name** field.

Selecting a color from the **Color** pulldown does not change the displayed color array or the **Name** field.

When you select a new color with either method, that color is displayed in the lower half of the sample color square until you select **Apply**.

◆ **Tip:** If you select a color from a library and then switch to another color model, the sliders in the new color model are set to match the color selected from the library. However, if you change colors using a color model, and then display a library, the library color display and Color pulldown do not change to match the selected color. To find the best available match in a library, use the Library slider to display an array of colors from the library that approximates the desired color. Select a close match from the array and use the sample color square to find the best match. You can fine tune the color by adjusting the tint.

Selecting Colors To Use in Documents

The *Color* dialog box allows you to select colors for fills and edges of graphics objects and for components and text:

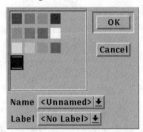

You can select any color square in the upper left of the dialog box. You can use the **Name** pulldown to select any color name/tint combination for which a name has been assigned (see page 175). With the **Label** pulldown, you can select any color to which you have assigned a label.

Pattern
Palette

Pattern Palette

The pattern palette permits you to change and delete the definitions of existing patterns and to define new patterns. Your changes to the pattern palette apply only to the current document, and to any document created as a copy of it.

You can copy patterns to create new ones, and you can cut or copy patterns and paste them between documents. Changes to the pattern palette take effect in the graphics fill pattern palette (see page 152) when the document is saved and reopened.

~ **Note:** Patterns are not exported from catalogs.

◆ **Tip:** A pattern that is cut or copied from a Pattern Palette Editor dialog box is placed on the clipboard as a "palette" icon and can be pasted directly onto the desktop. If you select and open this icon, you will see a Pattern Palette Editor dialog box containing only that color. You may modify the color, save and close the dialog box, and paste the icon into a Pattern Palette Editor dialog box. A "palette" icon looks like this:

A *Pattern Palette Editor* dialog box is opened:

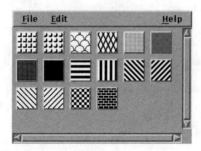

Creating and Deleting Patterns

All existing pattern definitions for the current document are displayed in the rows of squares. Any pattern may be selected for editing; selection causes the square to increase in size. To create a new pattern, copy and modify an existing one.

You can select a pattern and then execute Edit→Cut to remove it or Edit→Copy to copy it. A cut or copied definition can be pasted in this or another pattern palette by using one of the four options on the Edit→Paste submenu:

Edit→Paste→Before	This choice requires that a pattern be selected in the destination palette. The pasted pattern is positioned immediately before the selected pattern.
Edit→Paste→After	This choice requires that a pattern be selected in the destination palette. The pasted pattern is positioned immediately after the selected pattern.
Edit→Paste→Beginning	The pasted pattern is positioned at the beginning (upper left) of the rows of patterns.
Edit→Paste→End	The pasted pattern is positioned at the end (lower right) of the rows of patterns.

Modifying Patterns

A pattern is a 16 by 16 array of pixels, which is repeated as often as necessary to fill an area.

To modify a pattern, double–click on it, or click on it and select Edit→Open. The selected pattern's *Pattern Editor* dialog box appears:

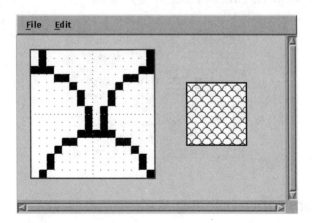

The large box on the left is a pixel-level diagram of one repeating unit of the pattern. If you click the left mouse button over a pixel on this diagram, the pixel turns black. If you drag the mouse while holding the left button down, all pixels over which the cursor passes turn black. Similarly, use the middle mouse button to turn pixels white. The small box on the right shows a sample area filled with the pattern, and is updated as you make changes.

File→Save applies your changes (you must execute File→Save from the *Pattern Palette Editor* dialog box and save the document to make them permanent).

Edit→Invert replaces black with white and white with black in the pattern.

Edit→Reflect→About Horizontal Axis mirrors the pattern across a horizontal line running through the pattern's center.

Edit→Reflect→About Vertical Axis mirrors the pattern across a vertical line running through the pattern's center.

Edit→Reflect→About Major Diagonal mirrors the pattern across a line running from its lower left corner to its upper right corner.

Edit→Reflect→About Minor Diagonal mirrors the pattern across a line running from its upper left corner to its lower right corner.

Edit→Rotate→Clockwise rotates the pattern 90 degrees in a clockwise direction.

Edit→Rotate→Counterclockwise rotates the pattern 90 degrees in a counterclockwise direction.

Edit→Rotate→Halfway rotates the pattern 180 degrees.

Modifying the Pattern Palette

Edit→Undo undoes the most recent change. Edit→Redo reverses the most recent Undo. If you make changes using the *Pattern Editor* dialog box and the pattern editor File→Save menu choice, *all* those changes made with the pattern editor are undone and redone as one change.

File→Save on the *Palette Editor* dialog box applies all changes; they are made permanent when you save the document. File→Apply makes changes available for setting the fill patterns of graphics objects (see page 152).

File→Save As allows you to save the entire palette as a separate desktop icon. It works the same as File→Save As on the *Color Palette Editor* dialog box (see page 176).

*Image
Editor*

Image Editor

The image editor permits you to make changes to raster (bitmap) images. You can "paint" on the images, crop them, and change the state of individual pixels.

The image editor is accessed by selecting an image file icon and opening it, or by opening a raster image within a frame in a document. An image editor window is opened:

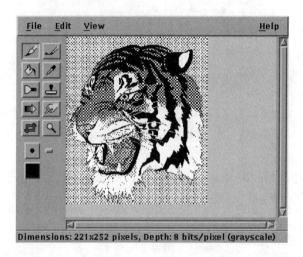

☞ **Note:** The image editor window for images in a document has additional features (see page 195).

The left side of this window displays a variety of tools, while pulldown menus appear across the top. The image is displayed in the remainder of the window; this area may be enlarged by making the window larger. If the image is too large to fit in the display area, the part of the image displayed may be selected using the sliders at the right and bottom of the window.

Pulldown Menus

File Pulldown

The File→Save menu choice saves the image in its current state, modifying the contents of the original file. With File→Save As you can create a new file to contain a modified image, leaving the original file unchanged. A *File Save* dialog box opens:

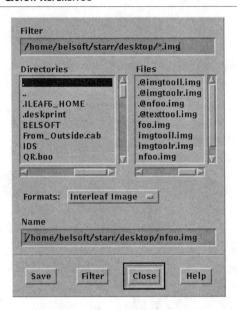

The name of the file that contained the original image is displayed in the **Name** field. You can alter the contents of this field by typing in it or by selecting a line in the **Files** list. When you select **Save**, the current state of the image is written to the file specified by the **Name** field. This may be a new file.

➾ Note: If the **Name** field contains the name of an existing file, including the original filename, selecting **Save** creates a new icon with the same name, and a new file.

The Formats pulldown lets you choose from among three raster image formats: Interleaf .img file (Mona Lisa icon, the default), Sun Raster, and X Window dump.

➾ Note: Any of the formats listed above may be opened directly by the image editor.

When you use File→Save As, the icon originally opened is closed, and you are editing the new icon. Subsequent save or revert operations pertain to the new file.

◆ Tip: If you use image editor File→Save As and the image you are editing is within a document, the image is saved to an image file (Mona Lisa icon). The document is not saved.

You can discard edits during a session without closing the image by using the File→Revert to→ submenu. File→Revert to→Saved loads and displays the most recently saved version of the image.

When you are editing a raster image that is within a document (in a frame), File→Revert to→Backup loads and displays the most recent backup version of the image. The backup version contains the contents of the image file at the time you opened the image editor for that image. When you close the image editor, that backup version is lost, although the version as of the time the document was opened can be retrieved with Revert to→Saved from the document menu bar **File** pulldown.

◆   **Tip:** The saved version of the image may be older than the backup version, since the saved version dates back to the most recent opening of the document, while the image may have been changed, closed, and reopened numerous times while the document has remained open.

If you are editing an image on the desktop (a Mona Lisa icon), File→Revert to→Backup has the same effect as File→Revert to→Saved. No backup file is created when a Mona Lisa icon is saved.

Edit Pulldown

The most recent change can be undone by selecting Edit→Undo. The undone change can be redone with Edit→Redo.

Edit→Clear sets the entire image (all pixels) to the current color.

Edit→Invert sets each pixel to the complement of its current color: black becomes white, and so forth.

View Pulldown

The View→Zoom→ menu choices allow you to display and edit an enlarged view of the image being edited. This makes it easier to accurately edit small details.

This submenu has the following choices:

Toggle	The zoom factor reverts to 100% if the image is currently enlarged, or to the most recent enlargement factor if it is currently displayed at 100%.
Larger	The zoom factor increases (zoom in).
Smaller	The zoom factor decreases (zoom out).

Percent	A *Zoom Percent* dialog box is opened:

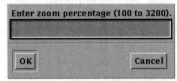

The operator can enter the desired zoom factor, which is rounded off to the nearest 100%.

Reset	The zoom factor is set to 100%.

The View→Rotate→ menus rotate the image in multiples of 90 degrees.

◦◦ Note: The display of the image is rotated, but the actual image is unaffected.

◦◦ Note: When you rotate an image, the part of the image that is displayed in the window remains the same, although it is rotated. Thus, you do not lose sight of your working area. If the image is larger than the window, the sliders are adjusted to compensate for the rotation.

View→Rotate→Clockwise rotates the image 90 degrees clockwise. View→Rotate→Counterclockwise rotates the image 90 degrees counterclockwise. View→Rotate→Halfway rotates it 180 degrees.

Brushes and Colors

Many image editor operations use a "brush." A brush is a special mode of operation of the mouse, in which pixels of the image change color as the mouse cursor passes over them. This is called "painting" the image. When the mouse cursor is operating as a brush, it can have a variety of sizes and shapes. The size and shape of the brush, as well as the path of the mouse, determine which pixels are affected by a given mouse movement when painting.

When painting, affected pixels take on the *current color* (or, optionally, its complement). This is true for black and white, gray scale, or color images, though the range of available colors naturally varies in each case. The current color is displayed in the lowest box on the left side of the palette. Clicking the select button on this box opens a color editor window (see page 174), allowing you to set the current color directly. As explained below, you can also set the current color by selecting a color displayed on the image.

In color images, there is a button to the right of the current color box. Clicking on this button opens a palette of 256 available colors. You can select any displayed color to be the current color by dragging the mouse to it. Unless you are using them all, many of these colors will be white. You can select any white color to make it current, then select the color box and modify the color using the color editor, effectively adding a color of your choosing to the palette.

Since there are only two possible colors in a black and white image, you cannot open a color editor. Clicking on the current color area toggles the current color between black and white.

On the left side of the palette, just above the current color box, are two selectable objects pertaining to the brush. Selecting the button on the right opens a palette of different brush sizes and shapes, which you can select by moving the mouse to the desired brush and releasing the select button. The button on the left displays the current brush size and shape. Selecting this button toggles the brush between the most recently selected size and shape, and a point (single pixel).

The palette of brush shapes and sizes can also be accessed during painting operations by pressing the right mouse button.

Available brush shapes include point, square, circle, and lines in various slants.

Tools

 Brush Tool

This tool allows you to "paint" within the image display area, using the mouse as a brush. With this tool selected, moving the mouse cursor with no buttons pressed moves the brush within the image; the image is not modified unless you press the left or middle button. The left button turns the mouse cursor into a brush that paints the current color. If you click the left button, a pixel, line, circle, or square in the current color is created in the image. If you hold this button down and drag the mouse, a continuous path in this color is created. The middle button turns the mouse cursor into a brush that paints in the complement of the current color (except in color images).

Autopickup Tool

This tool allows you to paint by extending the area filled with a given color. It automatically sets the current color to whatever color is under the mouse cursor when you press the left button (or, except in color images, the complement of this color if you press the middle button). As long as you hold the selected button down, you can continue to paint with this color. Whenever you press the left or middle button again, the current color is reset.

 Fill Tool

When this tool is selected, the cursor becomes a paint bucket icon. Move this cursor over the image, and click the left mouse button. All contiguous pixels that are the same color as the area under the cursor are filled with the current color. If you use the middle mouse button, the fill is done with the complement of the current color (except in color images).

◆ **Tip:** The precise location of the cursor is the lower end of the stream of paint being poured from the paint bucket icon.

◆ **Tip:** In a gray scale or color image, the number of contiguous pixels that are exactly the same color may be small, so the Fill tool may not have the intended effect – it may even appear to do nothing. Where an area of one color is bordered by solid shapes, the Fill tool can be a very efficient way to color the area.

▲ **Warning:** The Fill tool only affects the part of the image that is actually displayed in the editor window, so be careful not to overlook part of the image that you want to fill but that is beyond the edge of the display.

 Pickup Tool

The mouse cursor becomes an image of a medicine dropper. This tool sets the current color to whatever color is under the cursor when you press the select button. Then, you can paint with the current color by pressing the select button, or (except in color images) with its complement by pressing the middle button. You can carry out repeated paint operations with the same current color.

◆ **Tip:** The precise location of the cursor is the lower left end of the medicine dropper.

 Scraper Tool

When this tool is selected, the mouse cursor becomes a brush that "paints" the colors of the original image. Another way to state this is that the mouse "scrapes" away any changes, restoring old pixel values. Note that with this tool, unlike the other brush tools, the pixels affected by the brush need not all turn the same color.

The select button restores pixels to their state as of the last saved version, whereas the middle mouse button restores pixels to their state as of the time the image was opened for editing. Since the image may be saved several times in an editing session, the middle button may restore an older version than the select button.

As with other edits, changes made to the image using the Scraper tool do not take effect in the saved version unless you save the image.

 Clone Tool

This tool is used for copying any part of the image to any other part of the image. When you select the tool, the mouse cursor becomes a circle with crosshairs. Center this cursor on the part of the image you want to copy and press the select button again. The mouse cursor will be displayed with the size and shape of the brush, filled with black. If you click the select button again, the area covered by the brush will be painted with a copy of a similar sized area of the image centered on the point at which you clicked the mouse with the crosshairs displayed. If you hold the select button and drag the mouse, the area over which the brush passes is painted with a copy of the image centered on the same point.

If you drag the mouse far enough that the area being copied reaches an edge of the image, the mouse cursor (brush) will stop moving, because you cannot copy off the edge of the image.

◦ **Note:** The select button paints by copying from the image as most recently saved. The middle button works the same way, except that it copies from the original image (the image as you most recently opened it). Neither one copies changes you have made since the most recent save.

◆ **Tip:** By repeatedly moving the mouse a short distance and clicking it, you can "tile" an area with copies of a small part of the image. By holding a button down and dragging the mouse, you can copy an arbitrarily large fraction of the image onto any other area of the image.

 Fade Tool

The Fade tool (which is available only for eight-bit gray scale and 24-bit color images) darkens or lightens any part of an image. The mouse cursor takes the size and shape of the current brush. The left mouse button lightens an image and the middle button darkens it. Each click of a button lightens or darkens the area covered by the brush. Each time the brush is dragged over an area with a button pressed, the area the brush passes over is darkened or lightened. Each operation causes a slight change, so many repetitions may be needed to obtain the desired effect.

 Blend Tool

The Blend tool is available only for eight–bit gray scale and 24–bit color images. This tool adjusts the value of each pixel in the area covered by the brush toward the average of all pixels in the area covered by the brush. The effect after enough repetitions is that the entire area becomes the same shade of gray. Fewer repetitions allow you to soften transitions between adjacent areas. For example, if you have an image of text on a contrasting background, you can soften or blur the boundaries between the letters and the background.

The left mouse button controls the blending effect. The mouse cursor takes the size and shape of the current brush. Either clicking the left button repeatedly or holding it down and dragging the brush causes the fade effect on the area covered by the brush. While the left button is held down, the brush shows a complemented view of the area under the brush, enabling you to continually monitor the degree of fade.

 Crop Tool

This tool permanently removes part of the image from top, bottom, or either side. When this tool is selected, the mouse cursor becomes crosshairs. Move the cursor near a corner or edge of the image, and press the left (or middle) button. As you move the cursor toward the center of the image, you will see the image being cropped from the edge or corner at which you pressed the button. When you release the button, cropping ceases and the cropped image is displayed.

◆ **Tip:** To crop along one edge, select the crop tool, then place the crosshairs near the center of that edge and press the left (or middle) button to begin cropping. To crop along two adjacent edges at once, start with the crosshairs near the corner where they meet.

◆ **Tip:** For very accurate cropping, zoom the image using the View→Zoom→Larger menu choice before cropping.

◆ **Tip:** The Edit→Undo menu will reverse the effect of a crop if selected before any further edits are made.

Zoom Tool

When this tool is selected, the mouse cursor becomes a picture of a magnifying glass, similar to the tool icon. The effect of the tool is similar to that of the View→Zoom→Larger and View→Zoom→Smaller menu choices: clicking the left mouse button doubles the magnification, and clicking the middle mouse button reverses that effect.

◆ **Tip:** The Zoom tool has one major advantage over the View→Zoom→Larger menu choice: when you click the left mouse button, the part of the image under the mouse cursor will remain in view even when a large part of the image goes out of view due to magnification. You do not have to adjust the image position with the sliders to find the part in which you are interested.

Editing Images in a Document

When you open an image that is within a frame (as opposed to opening a Mona Lisa icon on the desktop), the image editor opens with this window:

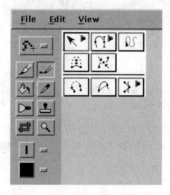

Note that an additional tool appears at the top of the tool icons. This tool can display one of three icons, providing three functions for use within frames. Holding the left mouse button down over this tool brings up a palette of the three icons.

When the drawing path icon is displayed, the other tools are active, and can be used to draw, fill, erase, and so forth.

If you select the "viewport hands" icon, all the other tools disappear, and a a scaled view of the image is displayed. This view is zoomed up or down so that the entire image is displayed in the available window size. This is useful in two ways:

Viewing the entire image	If the image is larger than the editor window, you can get an overview of the entire image at once.
Measuring any part of the image	By holding the left mouse button down while dragging the mouse, you can clip or enlarge the scaled view. This does not affect the image being edited. The dimensions in pixels of the magnified fraction of the image that is displayed at any time are listed in the status line at the bottom of the window:

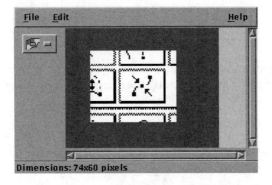

In the above example, the part of the image in the clipping box is 74 pixels wide and 60 pixels high.

If you select the intensity scale icon, the other tools disappear and two new tools are displayed, along with an intensity mapping graph:

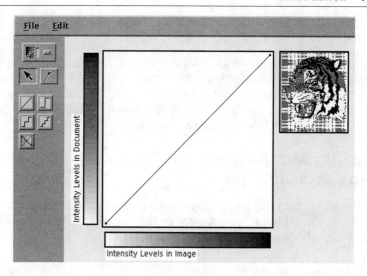

When you paste a raster image into a frame within an Interleaf 6 document, the image is stored separately from its representation in the document. The underlying image is "mapped" into the image object within the frame, meaning that the image's pixel data – whether black and white, gray scale, or color – is used to generate pixels at corresponding positions within the visible object in the frame.

Intensity mapping refers to the method by which pixels of the image data are mapped into pixels in the frame. By default, the intensities of the pixels in the image are mapped directly into the graphic object, with the result that the appearance of the image in the frame closely matches that of the underlying object. You can modify this mapping, reducing or increasing the intensity within the frame corresponding to a given intensity in the image. By completely inverting the mapping, you can effectively reverse foreground and background relationships: you can turn black text with a white background into white text with a black background.

◆ **Tip:** Changing the mapping does not change the underlying image data. It only changes its appearance within the frame. That is why the intensity mapping functions are available only with images within frames. When you change an intensity map, the image displayed in the main image editor window does not change. However, when you select File→Save in the image editor, the image depicted within the frame will change to correspond to the new intensity map.

The intensity mapping graph shows the mapping between the intensity levels of the image (vertical axis) and those in the frame (horizontal axis). A straight line from the lower left corner to the upper right corner represents the default mapping.

To the right of the graph is a small preview window, showing what the image looks like with a given intensity map. The view of the image displayed in the main image editor window displays the image itself, and is unaffected by the intensity map. The preview window lets you see what the image will look like in the document.

Intensity Mapping Tools for Color and Gray Scale Images

Of the following tools for modifying the intensity map, only the tools to restore the default map and to invert the map are available for black and white images.

 Arrow Tool

With this tool selected, you can use the left mouse button to select and drag any point on the intensity map. On the default map, as depicted, you can drag either endpoint. By dragging the left end to the top and the right end to the bottom, you invert the map.

 Point Tool

This tool allows you to create new points on the map, dividing the map up into smaller line segments. Select this tool, then click the mouse on the intensity graph. The location on which you click will become a point on the graph; whatever segment of the graph passes directly above or below that point will be broken into two segments to include the new point. You can then drag the new point with the arrow tool.

    **Specific Maps**

These tools set the intensity map to resemble the icon in each case. The first of these tools restores the default map.

 Inversion Tool

This tool inverts the map around a horizontal line. This reverses the mapping: the most intense image pixels become the least intense in the frame, and vice versa.

➥ **Note:** In color images, intensity changes are applied to the components of a color in a given color model. Reversing the intensity map has the effect of complementing all colors.

Chart
Editor

Chart Editor

About Charts

A chart is a graphical presentation of data. In Interleaf 6, a 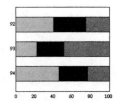 chart is one of the kinds of objects that you can create within a frame. To create a chart, first create a frame, then open the graphical tool palette (see page 135). On the tool palette, select the chart tool. Then move the mouse cursor into the frame, press the select button, and drag the mouse until your new chart has reached the desired initial size. Or, select Create→Chart on the document menu bar Create pulldown.

This is the appearance of a new chart:

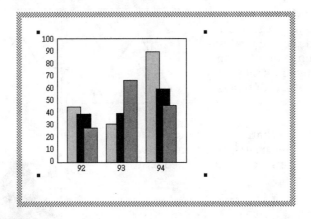

Note that the frame containing the chart is surrounded by a gray border, indicating that the frame is open, and that the chart has anchor points at each of its corners, indicating that the chart is selected. By selecting and dragging these points, you can resize the chart. By selecting the chart, you can drag it to new positions within the frame.

The chart depicted above is a **column bar chart**, which may be displayed in vertical orientation, as above, or positioned with the bars horizontal. Other basic types you can select are:

100% horizontal bar chart
Each bar represents three data values. The color zones within the bars represent the individual values.

Vertical bar surface chart
Each "step" represents three data values.
Each color zone within a step represents
one value. These charts may also be displayed in horizontal orientation.

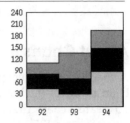

Pie chart
Each "pie" represents three data values.
Each color zone, or "wedge," within a
pie represents one value.

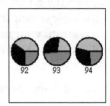

Line chart
Each point represents a
pair of 1.data values. Related points may be con-
nected by lines; there may
be several sets of points.

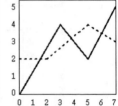

Line surface chart
Similar to line charts, except that the
area under a set of points is filled with
a fill pattern.

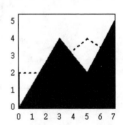

The Chart Editor

As described above, you can create, resize, and reposition charts using
the graphics tools. The chart editor lets you change the amount and
values of data displayed in a chart and to select from the available
styles and the options within each style.

To access the chart editor, open the frame containing the chart you wish to edit, then double-click on the chart. A *Chart Data* dialog box opens:

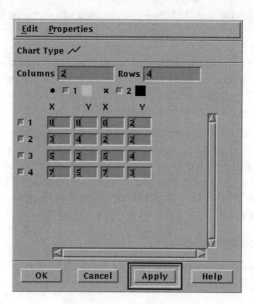

As described below, the fields on this dialog box vary, depending on the type of chart.

Chart editor functions fall into three basic groups. First is modifying the data values displayed, which is done using this dialog box. Second is editing, such as copying, deleting, and pasting data. This is done using the Edit pulldown menu in the menu bar of this dialog box. Last is changing the appearance of the chart, using the Properties pulldown menu of this dialog box.

Data Values

There are two distinct formats for chart data, used for different chart types. Therefore, two variations of the *Chart Data* dialog box are used.

All bar and pie charts use one data format, although the field names are different for bar and pie charts. In this format, data are organized in rows and columns. Each row has a label. A row corresponds to a cluster of bars identified by the row's label. Referring to the bar chart depicted on page 201, the rows are labeled 92, 93, and 94. A column corresponds to one bar in each cluster, always occupying the same position within the cluster. In the bar chart on page 201, all the black bars together are one column.

In a pie chart, rows are referred to as pies, and each pie has a label. Data values are wedges instead of bars, so each column corresponds to a single wedge from each pie.

Line charts also have data labeled as rows and columns, but their use is different because in a line chart, all data are *points*. A point consists of an X and a Y coordinate. This contrasts with other types of charts, in which a data value consists of a single number. In a line chart, a column is a set of related data points, which may be joined by line segments, as in the examples on page 202. A row contains one point in each column, with each point consisting of X and Y coordinates.

↦ **Note:** Line chart Y coordinates correspond to data values of bar and pie charts. X coordinates are not used in bar and pie charts. The row (or pie) labels of bar and pie charts are not used in line charts. As you change between the different types of charts, unused data in each case are not displayed, but they are retained and are displayed if you change to a type that does use them.

Bar and Pie Chart Data

When you double-click on a bar or pie chart, the following *Chart Data* dialog box opens:

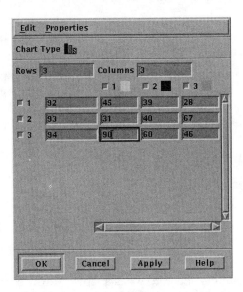

This illustrates the dialog box for a bar chart. For a pie chart, the field labeled **Rows** would be **Pies**, and **Columns** would be **Wedges**. You can change the number of rows (pies) or columns (wedges) by editing these fields.

The rows (pies) are numbered starting with 1. The field to the right of each number is a text field, which defines the label for that row or pie. The fields in the area to the right are all numeric data values. For a bar chart, they determine the relative heights or lengths of the bars. For a pie chart, these values determine the relative sizes of the wedges.

- **Note:** The bars or wedges are adjusted in size to fit nicely in the specified dimensions of the chart. If the chart is too small in relation to the range of values, the smaller wedges or bars may shrink to the point of disappearance.

- **Note:** If you convert a bar or pie chart to a line chart, the row (pie) labels will be retained but will not be displayed or used. The data values will become Y coordinate values for points in the line chart.

The toggle button to the left of each row number controls the visibility of that row. By default, each button is on, making the row visible. If you select a button, toggling it to off, that row's data values will turn gray. If you then select **Apply**, that row's cluster of bars, or pie, will be removed from the chart. The toggle button associated with each column has a similar function.

- ◆ **Tip:** You can make the data reappear by toggling the same button(s). You can select subsets of your data to view without losing any of the data. You can keep a large amount of data in a "master" chart and selectively display and print using copies of it.

Line Chart Data

The *Chart Data* dialog box for line charts is depicted on page 203. To open it, double-click on a line chart.

The fields labeled **Columns** and **Rows** display the number of columns (sets of related points) and rows (points in each column). You can change the number of points in the chart by changing these fields.

As with bar and pie charts, the rows are numbered at the left side of the dialog box, starting with 1. The button to the left of each row controls the visibility of the points in the row, as described above for row and pie charts.

The fields in the area to the right are all numeric. Each chart column has two columns of values, the X and Y coordinates of the points.

- **Note:** If you make the size of a line chart too small for the range of X or Y coordinates, some of the points may appear to overlap or may be squeezed into an edge or corner of the chart.

- **Note:** If you convert a line chart to a bar or pie chart, the X coordinates will be retained but will not be displayed or used. The Y coordinates will become the data values of the bar or pie chart.

The Edit Pulldown

The Edit pulldown lets you copy and paste data between charts and delete unused data from a chart.

The Edit→Copy menu choice copies the data area of a chart to the clipboard. Then, using Edit→Paste, you can paste this data into another chart. The effect is to overwrite the destination chart's data with the copied and pasted data. The numbers of rows and columns in the destination chart do not change. As much data as will fit in the destination chart is copied. If the destination has fewer rows or columns, excess data is discarded; if more, some data will not be overwritten.

∞ Note: Only data areas are copied. Bar or pie labels are not copied.

∞ Note: To copy and paste between a chart editor and another application, see page 209.

∞ Note: If copying from a line chart to a bar or pie chart, data values are copied from left to right in the order in which they appear. This means that X and Y coordinate values will alternate, and the result of the copy will probably not be useful. Similarly, values are copied from left to right in copying from a bar chart to a line chart, so that alternating values are used for X and Y coordinates. Again, the copy will probably not produce a useful result.

The Edit→Copy Special... menu choice opens a *Copy Special* dialog box:

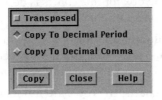

∞ Note: For the use of the **Decimal** buttons, see page 209.

Selecting the **Copy** button copies the chart's data area to the clipboard. By default, this has the same effect as the Edit→Copy menu item. If the **Transposed** toggle button is on, rows and columns are transposed as the data is copied to the clipboard.

The Edit→Paste Special... menu choice opens a *Paste Special* dialog box:

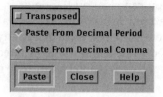

➥ **Note:** For the use of the **Decimal** buttons, see page 209.

Selecting the **Paste** button copies the data from the clipboard to the chart's data area. By default, this has the same effect as the Edit→Paste menu item. If the **Transposed** toggle button is on, rows and columns are transposed as the data is copied from the clipboard.

When chart data are transposed, the left-hand column becomes the top row, and the top row becomes the left-hand column. The effect is a rotation about the diagonal running from the upper left corner to the lower right corner. Values directly on the diagonal do not move.

For example:

1	2	3
4	5	6
7	8	9

A chart with these data values:

would produce these values when transposed:

1	4	7
2	5	8
3	6	9

You can achieve transposition by selecting **Transpose** on either the *Copy Special* or the *Paste Special* dialog boxes. If you select **Transpose** on both dialog boxes, both transpositions will be performed and they will cancel each other out.

➥ **Note:** When a chart's data area is transposed, the result is a data area that has the same number of columns as the original had rows, and vice versa. This transposed data area is then mapped into the destination chart's dimensions, just as in an ordinary copy and paste. If the two charts do not have the same numbers of rows and columns, the mapping will realign the data into rows and columns, and the result will probably not be useful.

◆ **Tip:** You can transpose a chart by copying and pasting it transposed into itself. However, if the chart has unequal numbers of rows and columns, the result will probably not be useful.

➥ **Note:** Transposing a line chart is similar to transposing a bar chart, except that points (pairs of X and Y coordinates) are transposed, rather than individual values. Each pair of X and Y coordinates remains as a pair after transposition.

With Edit→Delete, you can clear all the fields in the data area, or selected rows and columns. Edit→Delete→All Data clears all fields in the chart. Edit→Delete→Unused Data clears any rows and columns that have been turned gray using the associated toggle button (see page 205). The numbers of rows and columns do not change; fields are simply made blank.

◆ **Tip:** The Edit→Delete options take effect when you select the **Apply** button. If you wish to retrieve the cleared fields, select **Undo** after selecting **Apply**.

For line charts only, the Edit→Set Horizontal options allow you convenient ways to set X coordinate values where they follow a regular pattern, or follow the same irregular pattern for several different sets of values. This lets you establish regular intervals for values of independent variables. For example, you might establish a regular interval of years with the X coordinates, and then establish various values for each year as Y coordinates. Or, you might have year values that have irregular intervals, but you might have measurements in the same years for each type of data. You would still want to have identical X coordinates for each column.

Edit→Set Horizontal→Same Increment is used when the X coordinates have a regular interval. To use this option, enter the first two X values in the first X column, then execute Edit→Set Horizontal→Same Increment. The rest of the column will be filled out with values using the difference between the first two values as a regular increment. The resulting column of X values will be copied to the X values of all the other columns in the chart.

For example, if you enter this in the data area:

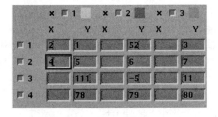

and then execute Edit→Set Horizontal→Same Increment, the result will be this:

If the X values do not have a regular increment, but should be the same for all columns, enter all the values in the left-most X column, and select Edit→Set Horizontal→Same Value. The left-most X column will be copied to the X values of all the other columns in the chart.

The Edit→Decimal Separator menus allow you to specify the character ("decimal point") to be used between the integer part and the decimal positions of numbers used to label chart axes. Edit→Decimal Separator→Period sets it to period, and Edit→Decimal Separator→Comma sets it to comma. In the data area of a chart, it is always a period.

Exchanging Text with External Applications

You can copy (or cut) and paste text between a chart editor and other applications. You can paste in either direction between an equation editor text window and an ordinary component in a document, or an Interleaf 6 host file. Depending on the capabilities of your operating system and other software, you may be able to copy and paste in either direction between a chart editor text window and a non-Interleaf application, such as a text editor.

To do this, use the chart editor Edit pulldown to **Cut**, **Copy**, or **Paste**, and the appropriate interface in the other application to paste, copy, or cut.

You can maintain the data that defines a chart in an external source, such as an ordinary Interleaf component or a separate text file, and paste it into a chart editor to publish it. This allows you to maintain the data using editors that may have features that you find preferable to those of the chart editor data window, or to initiate a chart by importing a table of figures.

↔ **Note:** Only data areas are copied. Bar or pie labels are not copied.

You may also use the *Copy Special* and *Paste Special* dialog boxes (see page 206) to move data between a chart editor and another application.

These dialog boxes permit you to control whether decimal points are indicated by periods (the default) or by commas in the other application. If you select **Copy To Decimal Comma**, and then paste the copied material, decimal points will be represented as commas in the pasted material. If you select **Paste From Decimal Comma**, commas in the source text will be converted to decimal points in the chart data.

⤙ **Note:** Commas or periods in the copied text that do not match the selected button on the *Paste Special* dialog box will be discarded, causing decimal fractions to revert to integers of larger magnitude.

In copying chart data and pasting it into an Interleaf 6 text component, each row becomes a separate line, ending with a hard return. Each data value is preceded by a tab. Copying from a component to a chart reverses the process.

If you copy a two by two bar or pie chart with this data area:

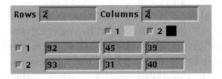

and paste it into an Interleaf 6 document as a top-level component, the pasted data will look like this:

45	39
31	40

If you copy a two by two line chart with this data area:

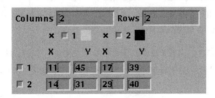

and paste it into an Interleaf 6 document as a top-level component, the pasted data will look like this:

11	45	17	39
14	31	29	40

The Properties Pulldown

The Properties pulldown has four choices: Style, Layout, Margins, and Axis. Each of the four choices opens a different page of a *Chart Proper-*

ties dialog box. At the top of each page is a row of radio buttons labeled **Style, Layout, Margins,** and **Axis,** which allow access to the other pages from any page. The Style page allows you to convert a chart to bar, line, or pie form and to set some variations on the appearance of each style. The Layout page controls gridlines and various aspects of the axes. The Margins page allows you to set margins for display of data and labels. The Axis page allows you to choose linear or logarithmic display of data and to control the numeric ranges of the axes.

The Properties Pulldown Style Page

This page has variations, displaying properties particular to the different chart styles. Each variation is depicted separately below. At the top of each variation are the radio buttons that allow changing to another page of the *Chart Properties* dialog box. Below these buttons are eight radio buttons for selecting chart style. These buttons are labeled with the following icons:

 Column bar chart

 100% horizontal bar chart

 Vertical bar surface chart

 Line surface chart

 Horizontal column bar chart

 Bar surface chart

 Line chart

 Pie chart

The Chart Properties Style Page for Bar Charts

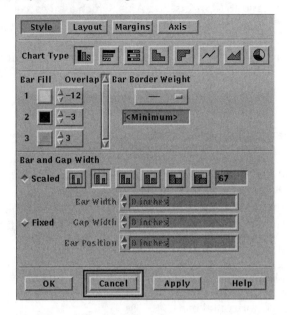

Bars are numbered beginning with 1, and listed in the upper left region. Each bar has independent fill and overlap properties. The fill property defines the color and pattern with which the bar is filled. Selecting the **Fill** button on a bar's numbered line opens a *Chart Fill/Edge Palette* dialog box:

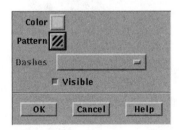

Click the **Color** button for access to a palette of colors. Use the **Pattern** button for a palette of available patterns.

The **Visible** toggle button controls whether the bar's fill will be displayed, as opposed to the bar being displayed as an empty shape the same color as the background. Turning this toggle off does *not* prevent the bar from being displayed.

◆ **Tip:** When you Apply changes on this dialog box, you must then select **Apply** on the *Chart Properties* dialog box before the changes will be visible in the chart.

The **Overlap** fields control the placement of bars to the left or right within each group of bars. Each field determines a number from -12 (far left placement) to 12 (far right placement). The numbers are in twelfths of a bar width. Overlap does not apply to bar surface charts.

◆ **Tip:** To obtain the standard appearance of a 100% horizontal bar chart, you must set all Overlap fields to the same value. Otherwise, the data values will appear as separate bars, not combined into one bar per group:

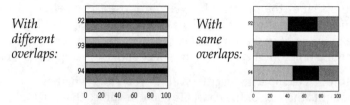

◆ **Tip:** Bars overlap within each group such that the bar numbered 1 is behind all other bars, etc. If you set a bar's overlap such that it falls entirely behind other bars, instances of that bar representing small data values may be entirely obscured. However, with positive data values, if two bars have the same Overlap value, they will be combined into a single bar (giving them different colors or fill patterns is recommended). This produces a variation on a 100% horizontal bar chart and is a good way to represent a lot of data within a small chart.

•◦ **Note:** Use of identical overlap settings for different bars with negative data values, except in 100% horizontal bar charts, is not recommended, because some data values (bars) may be completely obscured by others.

The **Bar Border** pulldown lets you choose the weight of the borders of the bars.

You can control the width and spacing of bars using the **Bar and Gap Width** area. There are two options, scaled (bars are evenly spaced across the axis) and fixed (you specify numeric parameters).

For scaled positions, select the **Scaled** radio button. You can now either select one of the radio buttons to the right of this button or select the numeric field to the right of the radio buttons. If you select one of the radio buttons, it determines the spacing relationships of bars and groups of bars. Buttons more to the left make narrower bars with more space between groups. Buttons to the right make thicker bars more tightly packed; groups may even overlap.

Each scaled spacing radio button causes a different value to appear in the field to the right, from 100 (narrow bars, loose spacing) to -15 (wide bars, tight packing). This number determines the gap width between groups as a percentage of the bar width; with this value, Interleaf computes how to allocate the length of the axis to bars and gaps. If this number is zero, there is no gap. If it is negative, there is overlap.

You can enter a desired value directly in the numeric field, including one outside the range provided by the radio buttons.

For fixed positions, select the **Fixed** radio button. Now you can enter three numeric values. **Bar Width** specifies the width of each bar. **Gap Width** specifies the distance between groups of bars. **Bar Position** specifies the distance from the chart origin to the first bar. This is the space to the right of the left-most bar, if the chart is in vertical orientation. For a horizontal chart, it is the space above the upper-most bar.

⊷ **Note:** Fixed spacing uses the values you enter whether or not the data fits the size of the chart. If you use values that are too large, some groups of bars may be "off the edge" of the chart and invisible.

The **Bar and Gap Width** controls apply to 100% horizontal bar charts even though the overlaps should be set to combine each group into a single bar. You can use these controls to make the bars thicker or thinner and to set the spacing between them.

The Chart Properties Style Page for Line Charts

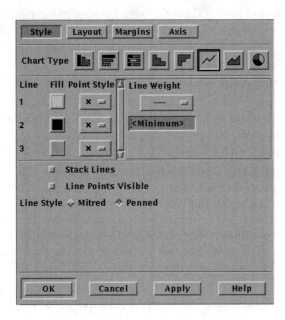

Lines are numbered starting with 1 to the left of this dialog box.

••• **Note:** The line numbers correspond to column numbers on the *Chart Data* dialog box, not to row numbers.

The **Fill** buttons open a *Chart Fill/Edge Palette* dialog box (see page 212). This lets you specify the color and pattern for fills on line surface charts, and for line segments connecting points on line charts.

◆ **Tip:** Fill patterns on line charts only take effect if the **Line Style** radio button for **Mitred** is on. When line segments are not very thick, large patterns will not be clearly seen, but small patterns such as dot screens work well.

••• **Note:** When you Apply changes on a *Chart Fill/Edge Palette* dialog box, you must then select Apply on the *Chart Properties* dialog box before the changes will be visible in the chart.

The Point Style pulldowns let you choose from a list of six available symbols to indicate the positions of data points on charts. Use the **Line Points Visible** toggle button to specify whether or not to mark points. The Line Weight pulldown controls the weight of the line segments used to connect points in each line (data column). If you choose <*None*>, there will be no line segments.

◆ **Tip:** If a line chart appears to be blank, you may have set line weight to <None> and turned **Line Points Visible** off, thereby suppressing display of both lines and points.

If the **Stack Lines** toggle button is on, Y coordinates for each line will be added to those of the preceding line. In other words, the Y value for each point of line 2 will be displayed relative to the Y value for the corresponding point of line 1, and so forth.

••• **Note:** If there are no Y coordinates less than zero, and all lines have the same set of X coordinates, then if **Stack Lines** is on, lines will never cross. For a line surface chart, this guarantees that no line's filled area will be obscured by any other line's area.

The **Line Style** radio buttons let you choose **Mitred** or **Penned** lines. Mitred lines have fill. Penned lines do not have fill, but can be dashed. You choose a dash pattern for each line with the **Dashes** pulldown of the *Chart Fill/Edge Palette* dialog box (see page 212).

The Chart Properties Style Page for Pie Charts

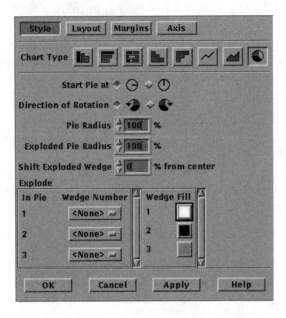

→ **Note:** Remember that each pie corresponds to one row on the *Chart Data* dialog box.

The first two lines control the positioning of the wedges. The **Start Pie At** radio buttons determine the placement of the first wedge of each pie. The left button starts the first wedge in the 3 o'clock position; that is, one border of the wedge will be horizontal and to the right of the center of the pie. The right button starts the first wedge in the noon position: one border will be vertical and above the center. Whether the first wedge lies clockwise or counterclockwise depends on the **Direction of Rotation** radio buttons. These buttons also determine the direction in which the wedges are placed around the pie, starting with wedge 1. Select the left button for counterclockwise rotation and the right button for clockwise.

The **Pie Radius** field lets you adjust the size of all pies in the chart. The default value, reflecting the initial composition of the chart, is 100. If you make it larger, all pies will increase in radius, to the point where they may overlap each other or their labels. If smaller, all pies will shrink.

You can select one wedge from each pie to be "exploded," that is, you can make one wedge distinct by changing its size or position in relation to the rest of the pie. This designation is made independently for each pie, using the Wedge Number pulldown for that pie in the **Explode in Pie** region. On this pulldown, select a wedge number (row number on the *Chart Data* dialog box), or <*None*> for no exploded wedge. The **Exploded Pie Radius** determines the radius of the exploded wedge as a percent of the radius of the pie. Note that as you change the radius of the pies, the exploded wedges maintain the same size ratio as long as you do not change **Exploded Pie Radius**. A positive value in **Shift Exploded Wedge** causes the exploded wedges to be moved out from the center of the pie, making them distinct without changing radius.

The **Fill** button for each wedge opens a *Chart Fill/Edge Palette* dialog box (see page 212), on which you can specify the color and pattern with which that wedge will be filled on all pies.

◆ **Tip:** When you Apply changes on a *Chart Fill/Edge Palette* dialog box, you must then select Apply on the *Chart Properties* dialog box before the changes will be visible in the chart.

The Properties Pulldown Layout Page

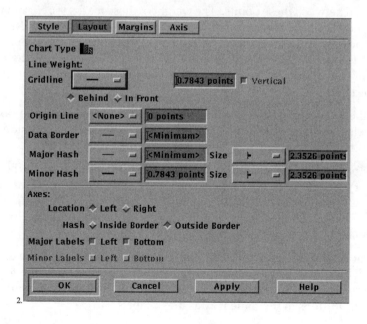

2.

All charts except pie charts can have gridlines and origin lines. Gridlines are regularly spaced lines that run from one edge of the chart to the opposite edge and demarcate values indicated on an axis. The weight of gridlines is determined by the Gridline pulldown. Select <*None*> to turn off gridlines. Whether gridlines are behind (obscured by) the data or in front of the data is determined by the **Behind** and **In Front** radio buttons.

On bar charts, gridlines are always perpendicular to the bars. On line charts, unless the Gridline pulldown specifies *<None>*, there are always horizontal gridlines. The presence of vertical gridlines is determined by the **Vertical** toggle button.

An **Origin Line** is a single line running from one edge to the opposite edge, indicating the origin (zero value point) of an axis. On bar charts, origin lines are always perpendicular to the bars. On line charts, origin lines are always horizontal. Origin lines do not appear on 100% horizontal bar charts.

The **Data Border** field controls the weight of the box drawn around the data area. Select *<None>* for no border.

The values along a labeled axis of a bar or line chart can be demarcated by hash marks. These are short vertical lines perpendicular to the axis. Major hash marks are positioned at the point on the axis that represents the value specified by each label. Minor hash marks are positioned between these points. The weight of these marks is determined by the **Major Hash** and **Minor Hash** fields, respectively. Select *<None>* for no hash marks. The Size pulldown for each type controls its length. The **Inside Border** and **Outside Border** radio buttons control whether hash marks are displayed inside the data border (where they may overlap the data) or outside.

In the **Axes** region, the **Location** radio buttons control whether the axis labeled with the Y coordinate values is on the left or the right side of the chart (this applies *only* to vertical bar charts and line charts).

For bar and line charts, **Major Labels** toggle buttons determine whether or not labels will be displayed on a vertical axis (**Left** or **Right**, depending on the **Location** buttons) and below the chart (**Bottom**). For pie charts, only the **Bottom** button is active, and it specifies whether or not labels appear beneath each pie.

Minor labels are available only for logarithmic axes (see page 221). They label values intermediate between integral powers of the logarithmic base. They are turned on and off by **Left**, **Right**, and **Bottom** toggle buttons in the same way as major labels.

The Properties Pulldown Margins Page

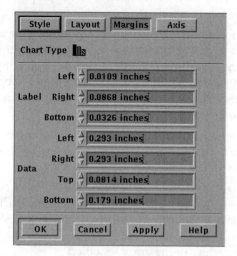

The **Label** group controls spacing around labels. The **Left** field applies only when the left side of the chart is labeled, as determined by the **Layout** field on the Layout page of this dialog box (see page 217). It specifies the spacing between the left edge of the data area and the right edge of the labels. If there are major hash marks outside the data area, as determined by the **Outside Border** button on the Layout page, the spacing is measured from the left edge of the hash marks to the labels. If this field contains a negative value, the labels will overlap the data area or hash marks.

The **Right** field applies if the right side of the chart is labeled. It measures the distance between the right edge of the labels and the right edge of the graphics object containing the chart.

The **Bottom** field specifies the distance between the top of the labels beneath the chart and the data area (for pie charts, from the labels to the bottom of each pie). If there are major hash marks outside the data area, as determined by the **Outside Border** button on the Layout page, the spacing is measured from the bottom of the hash marks to the labels.

➥ **Note:** The **Left** and **Right** label margins do not have symmetrical definitions: the **Left** field measures between the label and the chart, and the **Right** field measures from the label to the graphics object, away from the chart. Increasing the value in the **Left** margin field moves left-side labels to the left, toward the edge of the graphics object and further from the left border of the chart. In-

creasing the value in the **Right** margin field moves right-side labels to the left, away from the edge of the graphics object and toward the center of the chart.

Note: If hash marks are turned off by making their weight zero on
the Layout page, the position of left-side and bottom labels does
not change. If hash marks are turned off by making their length
zero on the Layout page, the label position changes. In other
words, the specified size of hash marks is used in the label margin
computation, even if the marks are invisible.

Note: If you set label margins or hash mark lengths so that labels
overlap the data area or extend beyond the containing graphics object, labels will not display or print properly.

The **Data** group controls spacing between the data area of the chart and
the edges of the graphics object containing the chart. Changing these
fields leaves the containing graphics object the same size, but stretches
or shrinks the chart. If these fields are negative, the chart may be
"clipped" at the edges of the graphics object.

Note: The **Left**, **Right**, and **Bottom** fields in the **Data** margins do
not allow for labels or hash marks. If these elements are present,
you must ensure that the margins are large enough for them to be
visible.

The Properties Pulldown Axis Page

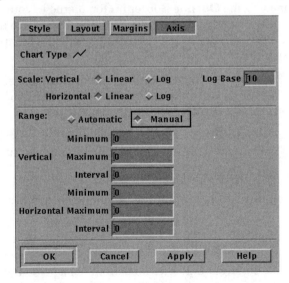

The **Scale** group allows a choice of linear or logarithmic horizontal and
vertical axes. These do not apply to 100% horizontal bar charts or to

pie charts. For other bar charts, only the axis parallel to the bars may be made logarithmic. For line charts, either or both may be logarithmic. If either or both of the **Vertical** and **Horizontal** lines has the **Log** radio button turned on, you can specify the logarithmic base in the **Log Base** field. The default base is 10.

The **Range** group lets you control the ranges of values represented by the chart axes. If the **Automatic** radio button is on, which is the default, Interleaf 6 computes the ranges of the axes to include all your data and fill the chart.

By selecting the **Manual** radio button, you can override the automatic ranges (not for 100% horizontal bar charts or pie charts). For bar charts, only the axis parallel to the bars may be adjusted. For line charts, the ranges of horizontal and vertical axes may be set. As a convenience, for bar charts, if you change back and forth between vertical and horizontal orientations, the **Horizontal** and **Vertical** groups of fields switch places and values, so that the applicable group is uppermost and one set of values is used.

◆ **Tip:** If you have a line or bar chart on which the data area has become empty, the cause may be that you have turned on **Manual** axes but not entered values in the **Horizontal** and **Vertical** fields.

The **Horizontal** and **Vertical** groups of fields each have three values. **Minimum** specifies the value of the end of the axis closest to the lower left-hand corner of the chart (or the bottom right, if the axis is to the right). **Maximum** specifies the value of the axis at the other end. **Interval** specifies the interval between labeled values, beginning with the specified minimum value.

◆ **Tip:** Setting ranges for your axes that omit part of your data causes the remainder of the data to fill the chart. This can be useful, especially for line charts, in giving you an amplified view of the selected part of the data. However, it can also cause you to inadvertently miss seeing part of your data.

Font Control

Within a chart, all axis labels, bar labels, and pie labels have the same font and point size. You can override the defaults with your own settings.

To make a change, open the frame, select the chart, and then apply changes as you would for ordinary text. You can use the Properties→Text... dialog from the document menu bar, or you can use the font, size, bold, and italic items on the document menu bar. You cannot use some text properties within charts, such as strikethrough and color.

Equation
Editor

Equation Editor

About Equations

An equation is one of the kinds of objects that you can create 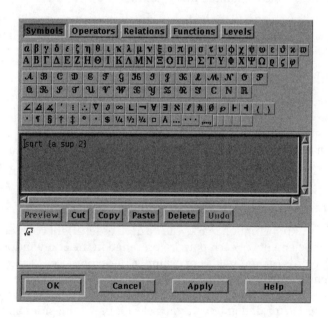 within a frame in Interleaf 6. To create an equation, first create a frame, then open the graphical tool palette (see page 135). On the tool palette, select the equation tool. Then move the mouse cursor into the frame and press the select button. Or, select *Equation* from the document menu bar Create pulldown with a frame open.

To open an equation editor, double-click on an equation within an open frame. An *Equation Editor* dialog box opens:

At the top of this dialog box are five radio buttons that control access to its five pages. Immediately below that is a section of selectable items that is different for each page of the dialog box. Next is the text window, in which you edit the text that defines the equation. Below the text window are a row of buttons, followed by the preview window, in which the equation is displayed in composed form, as it would appear in the document.

An equation is defined by the text in the text window. This text consists of any of the following:

- ▣ Keywords representing mathematical symbols, operators, relations, or punctuation, such as integral or root signs or parentheses
- ▣ Keywords representing functions, such as **sin** or **mod**
- ▣ String literals, such as variable names, that you define
- ▣ Numbers
- ▣ Keywords that control composition, such as *over*
- ▣ Font specifiers

When you modify the contents of the text window and press the **Preview** button, the modified equation is composed and the results are displayed in the preview window. **Apply** causes the changes to appear in the frame containing the equation.

Line breaks (returns) in the text of an equation are syntactically equivalent to spaces and may be inserted in place of spaces to make the equation easier to read.

The Elements of an Equation

When you select an item from the palettes at the tops of the **Symbols**, **Operators**, **Relations**, or **Functions** pages, the corresponding keyword is entered in the text window at the current text caret position. You can also type these keywords directly. String literals are easily entered between double quotes. Some of the items on the **Levels** palette are given special handling:

Parentheses and Brackets

A variety of punctuation marks can be used as left-right pairs. The left and right elements of each pair are preceded in the edit window with the keywords *left* and *right*. For example, the expression $x + y$ enclosed in parentheses would appear as *left (x + y right)*. You can select single elements of these pairs or complete pairs on the **Levels** page of the *Equation Editor* dialog box. If you select a pair, both sides appear in the text window, and you can enter any expression between them. The **Levels** page provides parentheses and a variety of brackets.

Curly braces ({ and }) can be used to group elements of the equation to achieve correct composition, without the braces actually appearing in the composed equation. When used this way, the braces appear in the equation text without the keywords *left* or *right*.

The equation editor will sometimes add curly braces to the text of an equation when you close and reopen it. This makes clear precisely how the editor is grouping the elements of the equation.

Piles

A *pile* is a collection of one or more elements that are arranged in a vertical stack. A pile is denoted by the keyword *pile* or one of its variants (see below). The elements of a pile can be any simple or complex equations elements, including piles. The elements must be enclosed in curly braces and separated from each other by the keyword *above*.

There are four compositional variations on the vertical stack of a pile. Each has its own keyword, as follows:

Keyword	Effect
pile	The elements of the stack are centered within the stack, and are tightly packed.
cpile	The elements of the stack are centered within the stack.
lpile	The elements of the stack are left-justified.
rpile	The elements of the stack are right-justified.

Matrices

A matrix is a series of elements, arranged horizontally, preceded by the keyword *matrix*, and enclosed in curly braces. Each element is equivalent to a pile and is enclosed in curly braces and preceded by a keyword. Within a matrix, special keywords denote the four types of piles as elements. They are *col*, *ccol*, *lcol*, and *rcol*, and create the same types of piles as *pile*, *cpile*, *lpile*, and *rpile*, respectively.

Strings

You may use any arbitrary string in an equation, such as a variable name. When you type such a string in the text window, select **Apply**, close the equation, and reopen the equation, the string appears within curly braces, with spaces between the digits. For example, *hours* would be converted to *{h o u r s}*.

If you enter a string between double quotes, it will not be placed between curly braces as described above, but will remain as you typed it.

◆ **Tip:** If you wish to use, as an element of an equation, a string that happens to be an equation editor keyword, you must enclose it in double quotes. For example, *hours + 5 + lcol* would produce a syntax error, but *hours + 5 + "lcol"* is valid syntax.

◂ **Note:** Numbers do not receive special treatment. A string of digits is handled the same as any other string.

The Editing Buttons

In the text window, you can select text by dragging the mouse with the left button held down. You can use the buttons to the right of the **Preview** button to **Cut** or **Copy** the selected text. With no selection, you can **Paste** what you have cut or copied. You can also **Delete** a selection, which does not allow you to copy it. **Undo** takes you back to the most recent **Apply**.

You can also paste material between the text window and other documents (see the next section).

Exchanging Text with External Applications

You can copy (or cut) and paste text between an equation editor and other applications. For example, you can paste material into another equation editor text window. You can paste in either direction between an equation editor text window and an ordinary component in a document. Depending on the capabilities of your operating system and other software, you may be able to copy and paste in either direction between an equation editor text window and a non-Interleaf application, such as a text editor.

To do this, use the equation editor **Cut**, **Copy**, or **Paste** buttons, and the appropriate interface in the other application to paste, copy, or cut.

You can maintain the text that defines an equation in an external source, such as an ordinary Interleaf component or a separate text file, and paste it into an equation editor to compose and publish it. This allows you to maintain the text using editors that may have features that you prefer to those of the equation editor text window. In particular, the equation editor text window removes all line breaks when an equation is closed and reopened, which makes it more difficult to edit large equations.

Font Control

When you create a new equation, all parts of it have the same font and point size. By default, anything you add to the equation will be in the same font and size. You can override these defaults for the entire equation or any part of it.

To make a change that applies to the entire equation, open the frame, select the equation, and then apply changes as you would for ordinary text. You can use the Properties→Text dialog from the document tool bar, or you can use the font, size, bold, and italic items on the document menu bar. You cannot use some text properties within equations, such as strikethrough and color.

To make a change that applies to only part of an equation, you can add font, size, and typeface specifications in the text window:

- ▣ To change font, use the keyword *font* followed by a font family name. The font name must be an Interleaf font family specification, such as *"wst:helvps."*

- ▣ To change size, use the keyword *size* followed by a number (point size). Use *size* followed by either *"+"* and a number to increase point size by the specified number, or *"-"* and a number to decrease size.

- ▣ To change to boldface, use the keyword *"bold."* To return to light-face, use *"boldoff."*

- ▣ To change to italic, use the keyword *"italic."* To stop using italic, use *"italicoff."*

Changes specified by keywords override changes to the font properties of the equation as a whole (the text properties of the graphics object).

- ◆ **Note:** Special characters (symbols) may not always be available in the current font. When this happens, a character may display (or print) as an inverted question mark within a rectangle: ⍰. For example, a degree sign (˚) may not be available in a Palatino or Times font, but may be available in Swiss or Thames. You can correct these situations by making an explicit font change for these characters.

- ◆ **Note:** Although keyword-specified font properties override those of the equation object, the properties of the equation object may still affect the appearance of the equation, even when you have fully specified the font properties of all characters. For example, the font size of the graphic object will not override the size of characters whose size you have specified, but can affect aspects of composition, such as the positioning of superscripts.

Each of the keywords described above applies only to the immediately following item in the equation. For example, if *size 12* is followed immediately by *"hours"* * *"rate,"* only the word "hours" is forced to be in 12 point type. If *size 12* is followed immediately by *pile {...}*, everything in the pile will be in 12 point type, unless there is an overriding size specification within the pile. Curly braces may be used to combine arbitrary elements of an equation so that a keyword will apply to all of them. For example, if *size 12* is followed immediately by *{"hours"* * *"rate"}*, all of "hours * rate" will be in 12 point type.

If several keywords are used in succession, such as *size 12 bold italic*, all of them apply to the next element of the equation following the keywords.

Examples

$int\ from\ 1\ to\ n\ sqrt\ x\ sup\ 2 + 1$ $\displaystyle\int_1^n \sqrt{x^2} + 1$

$x\ sup\ 2$ denotes the square of x and sup indicates a superscript.

$int\ from\ 1\ to\ n\ sqrt\ \{x\ sup\ 2 + 1\}$ $\displaystyle\int_1^n \sqrt{x^2 + 1}$

The curly braces following $sqrt$ do not appear in the composed equation, but they cause the entire enclosed expression to appear under the square root operator.

$\{int\ from\ 1\ to\ n\}\ \{sqrt\ left\ (\ \{x\ sup\ 2\} + 1\ right\ )\}$ $\displaystyle\int_1^n \sqrt{(x^2 + 1)}$

The left and right parentheses perform the same grouping function as the curly braces in the preceding example, and they are visible in the equation.

$\{left\ (\{a + b\}\ right\ )\}\ over\ \{left\ (\ \{c + d\}\ right\ )\}$ $\dfrac{(a + b)}{(c + d)}$

The curly braces around the $a + b$ and $c + d$ are not strictly required, but if they are omitted, there must be a space between the first left parenthesis and the letter a; otherwise there will be a syntax error and the a will not be visible.

$matrix\ \{lcol\ \{1\ above\ \{2\ 2\}\}$
$rcol\ \{"432abc"\ above\ \{5\ 6\ 7\}$
$above\ 6\}\}$

1	432abc
22	567
	6

This is a simple matrix with two columns, one of two elements, left-justified, and one of three elements, right-justified.

$bold\ \{left\ (\{a + b\}\ right\ )\}\ over$
$italic\ \{left\ (\ \{c + italicoff\ d - e\}\ right\ )\}$ $\dfrac{\mathbf{(a + b)}}{(c + d - e)}$

The upper part is bold. The lower part is in italic except for the letter d.

$size\ 18\ bold\ font\ wst:helvps$
$\{\{1\ 0\ 0\}\ sup\ size\ 8\ \{2\ 1\}\}$ $\mathbf{100^{21}}$

The entire equation is 18 point bold Helvetica, except for the superscript 21, which is 8 point. The size specification must be placed after sup; $size\ 8\ sup\ \{2\ 1\}$ is a syntax error.

Index

More
OnWord Press Titles

Pro/ENGINEER and Pro/JR. Books

INSIDE Pro/ENGINEER
Book $49.95 Includes Disk

Pro/ENGINEER Quick Reference,
2d ed.
Book $24.95

Pro/ENGINEER Exercise Book
Book $39.95 Includes Disk

Thinking Pro/ENGINEER
Book $49.95

Pro/JR. User's Guide
Book $49.95

Interleaf Books

INSIDE Interleaf
Book $49.95 Includes Disk

Adventurer's Guide to Interleaf Lisp
Book $49.95 Includes Disk

The Interleaf Exercise Book
Book $39.95 Includes Disk

The Interleaf Quick Reference
Book $24.95

Interleaf Tips and Tricks
Book $49.95 Includes Disk

MicroStation Books

INSIDE MicroStation 5X, 3d ed.
Book $34.95 Includes Disk

MicroStation Reference Guide 5.X
Book $18.95

MicroStation Exercise Book 5.X
Book $34.95
Optional Instructor's Guide $14.95

MicroStation 5.X Delta Book
Book $19.95

MicroStation Productivity Book
Book $39.95
Optional Disk $49.95

MicroStation Bible
Book $49.95
Optional Disks $49.95

Build Cell
Software $69.95

101 MDL Commands
Book $49.95
Optional Executable Disk $101.00
Optional Source Disks (6) $259.95

101 User Commands
Book $49.95
Optional Disk $101.00

Bill Steinbock's Pocket MDL
Programmer's Guide
Book $24.95

MicroStation for AutoCAD Users
Book $29.95 Optional Disk $14.95

MicroStation for AutoCAD Users
Tablet Menu
Tablet Menu $99.95

Managing and Networking
MicroStation
Book $29.95
Optional Disk $29.95

The MicroStation Database Book
Book $29.95
Optional Disk $29.95

The MicroStation Rendering Book
Book $34.95 Includes Disk

INSIDE I/RAS B
Book $24.95 Includes Disk

The CLIX Workstation User's
Guide
Book $34.95 Includes Disk

SunSoft Solaris Series

The SunSoft Solaris 2.* User's
Guide
Book $29.95 Includes Disk

SunSoft Solaris 2.* for Managers
and Administrators
Book $34.95
Optional Disk $29.95

The SunSoft Solaris 2.* Quick
Reference
Book $18.95

Five Steps to SunSoft Solaris 2.*
Book $24.95 Includes Disk

One Minute SunSoft Solaris
Manager
Book $14.95

SunSoft Solaris 2.* for Windows
Users
Book $24.95

Windows NT

Windows NT for the Technical Professional
Book $39.95

The Hewlett Packard HP-UX Series

The HP-UX User's Guide
Book $29.95 Includes Disk

The HP-UX Quick Reference
Book $18.95

Five Steps to HP-UX
Book $24.95 Includes Disk

One Minute HP-UX Manager
Book $14.95

CAD Management

One Minute CAD Manager
Book $14.95

Manager's Guide to
Computer-Aided Engineering
Book $49.95

Other CAD

CAD and the Practice of
Architecture: ASG Solutions
Book $39.95 Includes Disk

INSIDE CADVANCE
Book $34.95 Includes Disk

Using Drafix Windows CAD
Book $34.95 Includes Disk

Fallingwater in 3D Studio: A Case
Study and Tutorial
Book $39.95 Includes Disk

Geographic Information Systems/ESRI

The GIS Book, 3d ed.
Book $34.95

INSIDE ARC/INFO
Book $74.95 Includes CD

ARC/INFO Quick Reference
Book $24.95

ArcView Developer's Guide
Book $49.95

INSIDE ArcView
Book $39.95 Includes CD

DTP/CAD Clip Art

1001 DTP/CAD Symbols Clip Art
Library: Architectural
Book $29.95

DISK FORMATS
MicroStation
DGN Disk $175.00
Book/Disk $195.00

AutoCAD
DWG Disk $175.00
Book/Disk $195.00

CAD/DTP
DXF Disk $195.00
Book/Disk $225.00

Networking/LANtastic

Fantastic LANtastic
Book $29.95 Includes Disk

The LANtastic Quick Reference
Book $14.95

One Minute Network Manager
Book $14.95

OnWord Press Distribution

End Users/User Groups/Corporate Sales

OnWord Press books are available worldwide to end users, user groups, and corporate accounts from your local bookseller or computer/software dealer, or from HMP Direct: call 1-800-223-6397 or 505-473-5454; fax 505-471-4424; write to High Mountain Press Direct, 2530 Camino Entrada, Santa Fe, NM 87505-8435, or e-mail to ORDERS@ BOOKSTORE.HMP.COM.

Wholesale, Including Overseas Distribution

High Mountain Press distributes OnWord Press books internationally. For terms call 1-800-4-ONWORD or 505-473-5454; fax to 505-471-4424; e-mail to ORDERS@IPG.HMP.COM; or write to High Mountain Press/IPG, 2530 Camino Entrada, Santa Fe, NM 87505-8435, USA. Outside North America, call 505-471-4243.

Comments and Corrections

Your comments can help us make better products. If you find an error in our products, or have any other comments, positive or negative, we'd like to know! Please write to us at the address below or contact our e-mail address: READERS@ HMP.COM.

OnWord Press
2530 Camino Entrada, Santa Fe, NM 87505-8435 USA